Ethical Education in American Public Schools

by Waldo Beach

Reference & Resource Series

nea PROFESSIONAL LIBRARY
National Education Association
Washington, D.C.

Printing History
    First Printing: April 1992

Note

The opinions expressed in this publication should not be construed as representing the policy or position of the National Education Association. Materials published by the NEA Professional Library are intended to be discussion documents for educators who are concerned with specialized interests of the profession.

Library of Congress Cataloging-in-Publication Data

Beach, Waldo.
    Ethical education in American public schools / Waldo Beach.
       p.   cm. — (Reference & resource series)
    Includes bibliographical references (p.).
    "Stock no. 1540-1-00."
    ISBN 0-8106-1540-1
    1. Moral education — United States. I. Title. II. Series.
LC311.B39   1992
370.11'4—dc20   91-8463
                                            CIP

CONTENTS

The Author

Waldo Beach is Professor Emeritus at The Divinity School, Duke University, Durham, North Carolina

The Advisory Panel

Peter F. Carbone, Jr., Associate Professor of Education, Duke University, Durham, North Carolina

Wilhelmenia Cater, Social Studies Teacher, Elm Place Middle School, Highland Park, Illinois

Wolfgang Kuenzler, Social Studies Teacher, Bloomfield Junior High School, Connecticut

Jeannie Merkooloff, Instructor of History and Psychology, Fairleigh Dickinson University, Rutherford, New Jersey

Joyce Temby, Spanish and Mathematics Teacher, Los Cerros Middle School/Monte Vista High School, Danville, California

PREFACE

The intent of this brief volume is to analyze one of the most serious problems plaguing American public education today, namely, the ethical issues and dilemmas that permeate the life of our schools. It is addressed to teachers, counselors, coaches, and school administrators, especially those at the secondary school level, who are confronted daily with the thorny problems of student behavior in and outside the classroom. It is also directed to parents of school-age children who are—or should be—concerned with the moral nurture of their children and who may be led to cooperate with teachers and counselors in the cultivation of responsible behavior.

One basic premise of the book should be clearly set out at the start. Both descriptive and normative dimensions of the problems are discussed herein. "Descriptive" writing attempts as accurately as possible to describe the facts of the matter. "Normative" attempts to prescribe measures and policies that will provide helpful guidelines for what ought to be done. The descriptive and the normative—the "is" and the "ought"—should be held in sight together in the search for possible realistic solutions.

Experts in child psychology and educational theory have written a vast jungle of literature on moral education. I can give only limited attention to this. My own field of professional work has been as a teacher of ethics, more particularly Judeo-Christian ethics, in a university setting, which is far away from the rough and tough problems of an inner-city public high school. My academic myopia has been corrected by wisdom from some teachers and counselors "in the trenches," who have offered corrective suggestions. In particular I would like to thank Elnora Shields, Nancy Fulcher, Gail Hudson, Dr. Sheila Breitweiser, and the staff of the Durham County School Board for assistance. Also words of thanks are due to Duke University for research grant assistance and to Gail Chappell for expert clerical help.

Chapter 1

THE TATTERED FABRIC OF CIVIL COMMUNITY IN AMERICAN PUBLIC EDUCATION

Most Americans, whether parents of school-age children or not, enjoy the pleasant illusion that our schools are happy havens of civility, that students in the classrooms are models of docile decorum and modest propriety. But the reality is far from that comfortable fantasy. In recent years we have been jarred by alarming news accounts of a serious deterioration of moral standards and practices in our schools. These report not only headline-grabbing accounts of rapes of teachers by high school students, of violent clashes of racial gangs, and of drug trafficking on school grounds. There is also a pervasive breakdown in responsible and civil behavior, both in and out of the classroom. This is most evident in our impoverished inner-city schools, but the malaise also infects at an alarming rate the schools of rural and suburban America. This deterioration cannot be indexed on a quantitative scale, like SAT scores, but it is apparent that the rate of *moral* literacy is in sharp decline.

THE MAIN TROUBLE SPOTS

One area of serious trouble is the increased use, buying, and selling of drugs and alcohol, not only in senior high schools but in junior high and middle schools as well. According to one study,

illicit drug use in the United States is greater than in any other nation in the developed world. In 1985, about 54 percent of high school seniors used marijuana at some time, . . . and approximately 40 percent used some illicit drugs other than marijuana. . . . Cocaine today poses a significant threat to public health. In addition, more than 20 percent of American

7

teenagers smoke cigarettes and almost 6 percent are daily users of alcohol.[1]

A 1989 study by the Carnegie Council on Adolescent Development, *Turning Points: Preparing American Youth for the 21st Century,* reports that "92 percent of the high school class of 1987 had begun drinking before graduation; of those, 56 percent had begun drinking in the 6th to 9th grades and 36 percent in the 10th to 12th grades. These data do not include those who dropped out before graduating," for whom the percentage is much higher.[2] The use of hard drugs is found largely in the depressed areas of the inner cities, but it is spreading to suburban and rural areas. One drug currently in use is "speed." Another, "crack," is a cheaper form of cocaine than the straight substance; still, a small vial costs at least $3. With the recently increased "war on drugs" by local school officials, however, even crack is becoming more costly. This means that teenagers in school or out who are hooked on this drug must resort to break-ins and theft, even prostitution, to buy it.[3] Alcohol remains the major problem, however, as the statistics on arrests and tragic accidents and fatalities from drunk driving will attest.

Drug abuse in another form is the increased use of steroids by high school athletes who seek that extra edge of energy to win the game. Although one Olympic athlete in the 1980s was disqualified after testing positive for steroid use, few high school players are even tested for steroids. Even fewer are barred from playing.

A second trouble spot is that of widespread theft and deceit. Students steal food and lunch money from each other, as well as as property from school lockers. Plagiarism in writing exams and papers is also a common practice. The 1976 scandal at West Point, where some 150 cadets were dismissed for violating the Honor Code on a take-home exam and many others were implicated,[4] is but one instance that could be duplicated many times over in institutions of higher learning and in secondary schools as well. In addition, many prosperous term-paper "factories" sell their products for a handsome fee. These enterprises enable hard-pressed students who have three research papers due next week to slide by course requirements on the pretense that the paper is the product of their own research.[5] And in some schools, it is not uncommon for the grades of skilled athletes with poor academic records to be "fixed," for a fee, to assure their place on the team.

A third area of marked change in social behavior and moral standards has to do with sexual practices. Sexual intercourse outside marriage has been going on for many centuries, to be sure, but recent studies and surveys indicate an increasingly open and permissive attitude toward sexual practices. A Gallup poll of full-time college students published in *Newsweek* reveals statistics indicating a considerable change from the ethics of Puritan days. The data:

Have you ever engaged in sexual intercourse?

	Total students	Male	Female
Yes:	68%	76%	59%

When did you first engage in sexual intercourse?

	Male	Female
In college:	21%	32%
Before entering college:	77%	65%

Among those who had had sexual intercourse, 50 percent of the males and 47 percent of the females expressed no feeling of guilt or regret about their behavior.[6] According to the Carnegie Council report, "more and more teenagers below the age of 16 are becoming sexually active, become pregnant and give birth to low-weight babies. These young mothers tend to drop out of school early," with dire prospects for their future.[7]

One of the most disturbing developments in sexual practices among teenagers, whether they are enrolled in high schools or have dropped out, is the sharp rise in teenage pregnancies. The Alan Guttmacher Institute, which conducts the most extensive research on this problem, reports that the United States has the highest teenage pregnancy rate in the developed world: "An estimated four out of ten American women become pregnant in the course of their adolescent years. About 10,000 babies a year are born to children under the age of 15."[8] Even the current scare about AIDS has not yet served to reverse this trend.

A host of dark cultural, economic, and ethical factors lie behind these bare statistics. The consequences are sobering indeed. A large number of these young people are poor Black girls, living in the depressed parts of the cities. "Sixty percent of all Black babies today are born to never-married single mothers and two out of three children in Black female-headed households (67.1 percent) are poor."[9] Often these mothers have no parental support to help them take care of their children. If they do not have an abortion, their decision to keep the baby may be motivated by the sense of self-worth that motherhood provides. They may feel that self-worth is a commodity that is denied them by the economic and cultural circumstances in which they live. More often than not, the father of the infant has gone off, or if he is still around as "boyfriend," he has no income to assist in making ends meet. So the young mother must drop out of school and fend for herself as best she can, depending on her own parents, if possible, or on social welfare. The infant is raised in pitiful poverty, hardly the warm security of the conventional televised image of the American home. This phenomenon, of course, has noting to do with skin color. It is a function of the socioeconomic condition of poverty.

A fourth trouble spot, closely related, is in the area of race relations. Since *Brown v. Board of Education,* public schools are by law racially integrated. Recently when a group of white students appeared on the grounds of a North Carolina high school wearing Confederate symbols on their jackets and displaying a Confederate flag (causing their brief suspension by school authorities), this seemed to some a silly adolescent prank. To others, however, it was but one sign of a rising tide of racism.

Public schools are racially integrated in a formal sense. But sensitive teachers, by drawing on the talents of Black and white students in a drama production or school chorus, can observe the racial barriers and stereotypes, and change the relationship from interracial to interpersonal. To a great extent, however, informal segregation in community relations often prevails in the cafeterias and hallways. As one high school teacher put it, "Integration ends at 3 o'clock, when school is out." School yard fights and violence between Black and white "gangs" recently reported from South Boston and Chicago are on the increase. There are danger signs also of increased anti-Semitism and brawls between Caucasian and Hispanic or Asian-American students.

These facts and trends raise serious problems for principals and teachers responsible for school discipline. What are the legitimate modes of punishment for flagrant misbehavior? How can school authorities work to change the implicit or explicit rules of civil relationships to instill a sense of moral responsibility and conscience in the students of today's troubled schools? Is the purpose of schooling in America the acquisition of technical skills or the highest possible SAT scores? Or is it the development of character and conscience in training for responsible behavior in a civilized society? What is the role of the family and other institutions in society, especially those who have access to the child in the early years, even before kindergarten? In fact, students are enrolled in public schools after most behavior patterns have been firmly entrenched.

NINETEENTH CENTURY SCHOOL CULTURE

In citing these most visible trouble spots, we must avoid a Norman Rockwellian romantic delusion that this abuse of persons and property is unique to the schools of the latter part of the twentieth century, or that the schools of yesteryear were all models of piety, propriety, and decorum. To go back earlier, to Puritan days, at Harvard's first commencement in 1642 complaint was made against two young men, "of good quality, lately come out of England, for fond misbehavior, in swearing and ribaldry speeches, etc." The board gave the president authority to flog the students; this was done as soon as the exercises were over.[10] The present generation of school children holds no monopoly on mischief. Yet if one looks at the content of the curriculum of public schools of the nineteenth century, it is not a nostalgic delusion to acknowledge that moral education was a central purpose of the curriculum. Under the leadership of Horace Mann, the public school movement had a profoundly religious and ethical intent, albeit nonsectarian, under the terms of the First Amendment. Instruction "sought to form a sincere piety directed toward the Creator, a morality based upon the example and ideas of Jesus Christ and conducive to civic peace and social righteousness"—that was Horace Mann's ideal.[11]

This generalization about the moral and religious purpose of common education is confirmed by a look at the content of *McGuffey's Readers,* the standard fare in American public schools well into the early part of this century. Some 120 million copies of these texts were sold between 1836 and 1920, outsold only by the Bible and Webster's Dictionary.[12] In some schools today, under strong pressure from conservative religious parents, these *Readers* are coming back into use. Although the later revised editions watered down somewhat the high Calvinism of McGuffey's original forms, all editions were drenched with lessons in piety and righteousness. The qualities of character extolled most frequently are "charity, industriousness, patriotism, kindness, and piety."[13] The echo of this Protestant moral ideal may still be heard in the Boy Scout pledge dutifully repeated even to this day: "A scout is trustworthy, loyal, helpful, friendly, courteous, kind, obedient, cheerful, thrifty, brave, clean, and reverent." Although joining a Boy Scout troop is voluntary, not compulsory, many public school students are members and repeat this pledge.

Moral education—the nurture of conscience and character—was thus once as much the central purpose of the public school movement as it was of the private schools under church auspices. And at the upper levels in colleges established and sustained by various churches in the nineteenth century, the integrating course in the curriculum was the senior course in moral philosophy, taught by the college president who was usually a clergyman.

THE NEW CULTURE

How might we account for this deterioration of moral standards and behavior in our schools, this tattering of the fabric of civil community, this loss of integrity, accountability, mutual trust and respect that are the sinews of any healthy society?

To search within the walls and halls of the classrooms for the villains of this story would be a myopic and futile exercise. What we have described are the reflections of the powerful demigods of our contemporary secular culture. The real troublemakers of this piece are not mischievous children or insensitive teachers, but the forces of a materialistic, capitalistic, and technocratic culture that invade the school in countless ways to celebrate a lifestyle very different from that which *McGuffey's Readers* supposedly nurtured. Currently, the purpose of education has drastically changed from the nurture of conscience and character to the pragmatic purpose of equipping our citizenry with the skills necessary to cope within a technological society and to "make good" in a materialistic sense. The virtues of the Boy Scout credo have been replaced by the new syndrome of values that constitute the "good life": power, speed, comfort, efficiency, and sensual enjoyment, all under a halo of a narcissism that puts "me" first.[14] We may harbor the romantic notion that education changes societal structures and values, but in truth the demands of a materialist and technological society change the character of education.

This generalization about the sharp changes in the basic moral values in society at large and that infiltrate our school has been the subject of much scrutiny by sociologists and analysts of American culture, including Theodore Roszak, Robert Bellah,

Victor Ferkiss, Alvin Toffler, and Christopher Lasch. These writers all concur in pointing to several major forces that have changed the moral scenery and thereby the content of education.

The first factor of profound impact on the morale and the morality of school children is the radical change in the American family structure. Currently, 1 out of 2 marriages ends in divorce, as contrasted to 1 out of 37 in 1870. According to a recent study,

Of every 100 children born today:
  20 will be born out of wedlock.
  12 will be born to parents who divorce before the children reach 18.
  6   will be born to families in which one parent will die before the children reach 18.
  40 will live in female-headed households before adulthood.[15]

Also, the large extended family, with grandparents, parents, and children living in one household, and quite likely relatives nearby, is an endangered species. Families are scattered. This has a profound negative impact on children in terms of rootedness and security.

Within these cold statistics stand persons, young and old, with tensions and traumas of all kinds, especially acute for children, troubled and torn in their affections between their divorced parents, or knowing only one parent. These troubles children carry to school with them. Sometimes they push young people over the precipice of despair, leading to suicide or frequently to an escape from the harsh reality of homelessness by a "trip" on drugs or alcohol. Where family ties are broken, for many children their only sense of value is what they can "hold on to." Material things tell them what they are worth.

Therefore, though the TV screen portrays a pleasant image of the strong and happy American home in suburbia, where Mom, Dad, and the two children are enjoying a barbecue around a swimming pool, or rejoicing in the lovely home found for them by a national realty company, the reality is far from that lovely picture.

A second factor is the enormous impact of commercial TV. There have been many recent studies of the impact of TV upon youth. Ninety-eight percent of American homes have a TV set that is turned on about six hours every day, mostly to commercial channels. And VCRs have increased TV viewing. Children of school age watch TV about 30 hours a week. There is an inverse ratio between the amount of time they spend watching TV and their academic achievement in school. Not surprisingly, there is a proven correlation between televised aggression and aggressive behavior of school children.[16] What are they watching? TV has extended the horizons of vision to enable one to see what is happening in the global community: that is a clear moral benefit. On the other hand, the media concentrate on the sensational. This narrows the moral vision of the viewer. Moreover, the visual image strikes more at the emotions than at the mind. For the most part, these young viewers are looking at scenes of violence, sexual enjoyment, domestic bickering, or the heavenly bliss of whizzing down an open highway in a new and expensive car. The life abundant consists in the high consumption of goods that give one a "trip." Outward appearance counts for more than inner character. As John Silber of Boston University remarked, "The gospel preached during every television show is 'You only go around once in life, so get all the gusto you can.' It is a statement about theology; it is a statement about beer."[17] Whether through sitcoms or commercials, the message is the same. The golden rule seems to be: "If it makes you feel good, do it." Is it so strange then to find increasing incidents of sexual exploitation, of drug addiction, of violence?[18]

Still another powerful demigod influencing American culture and ethical behavior is a product of the scientific revolution—technology. Whereas the official mottos and rituals of America may speak of one nation, "under God," or "In God we trust," as if to say we live in a theocracy, the truth is that we live in a technocracy, where our ultimate trust is in the machine.

15

The real hidden creed of the average American is not "I believe in God the Father, Son, and Holy Spirit," but I believe in God the Father, Science, the Son, Technology, and in the Holy Spirit of Efficiency. Machines, the computer, the atomic weapon, the laser beam, the VCR, the X-ray, the tractor, the new miracle drug—these are our true saviors from death and destruction.

The technological revolution has had a profound influence on education at every level. Whereas, as we have noted, the aim of education in earlier eras was to cultivate piety and moral character, the current aim of education is to equip persons with the tools and skills necessary to cope efficiently within a technocratic culture. Witness the expansion of science courses in the curriculum and the shrinkage of the humanities courses in the universities and schools. Witness the marked increase in technical colleges and institutes and the decline of church colleges. Witness the trend in liberal arts colleges for students to major in subjects that will earn them admission into business, engineering, law, or medical schools. Under this ethos a sensible high school senior will elect a course in cosmetology rather than a course in philosophy studying Plato's cosmology. The former will help the student get a job, the latter would be useless. The countermeasures of Mortimer Adler's *Paideia Proposal* calling for a recovery of some of the classical elements of education go unheeded.

Where the chief end of the educational process is seen to be the acquisition of skills to run our machines of transport or office management with the highest possible degree of efficiency and speed, the classical ethical ends are neglected. A technocrat will say, "If we're technically capable of doing this, let's do it." The person of humane conscience will ask first: Will this technical skill serve to improve or worsen the human condition?" The answers, of course, are never a simple yes or no, but the ethical consideration and a caring responsible conscience should play a crucial part in the decision. In other words, the preoccupation with *how to* should not preclude a consideration of *what for*. As the National Commission on Excellence in

Education expressed it in *A Nation at Risk,* "An overemphasis on technical and occupational skills will leave little time for studying the arts and humanities that so enrich daily life, help maintain civility, and develop a sense of community. Knowledge of the humanities . . . must be harnessed to science and technology if the latter are to remain creative and humane."[19]

A sharp essay in *Time* pointed up the tragic and ominous incidence among high public officials of betrayal of public trust—in sleazy acts of deceit, cover-up, perjury, and flagrant violation of law. First there was Watergate. Then the Iran-Contra affair, Oliver North, the scandals surrounding the attorney general during the Reagan administration—the most notorious instances of actions that seem to pollute our political atmosphere—led to this *New York Times* editorial judgment, "As one scandal after another unfolds, it is clear that President Reagan presides over one of the most corrupt administrations ever."[20]

When prominent televangelists who presume to preach the Christian gospel of righteousness are caught in sex scandals or engage in racketeering to build lavish castles of affluence for their own use, they can hardly be regarded as role models for the nation's youth in our schools. The role models and heroes of today's youth are not government officials or civil rights leaders. In fact, they are the rock stars or the TV and movie celebrities. Part of the moral villainy here would seem to lie in the worship of mammon. The health of our capitalistic economy is vitiated by the insidious pursuit of wealth that cuts corners across the lawns of honesty or sneaks in stealth between the lines of the law in pursuit of affluence. This materialistic ethic penetrates the educational systems, at both lower and higher levels in subtle and disturbing ways.

Compare a sentence from President Kennedy's inaugural address, "Ask not what your country can do for you, but what you can do for your country," with Ronald Reagan's campaign appeal in 1984, "Ask yourself: Are you better off now than you were four years ago?" This is but a flash signal of a profound change in the moral climate of American culture, a shift from the strong sense of corporate responsibility, which de Tocqueville found characteristic of American life in the nineteenth century, to the me-centered individualism prevalent today. This is the ethos and lifestyle that Robert Bellah carefully documents in his *Habits of the Heart: Individualism and Commitment in American Life*.[21]

All these disintegrating forces pose formidable problems for educational administrators and principals, for school boards, for parents of children in school, and especially for the teachers working daily in the trenches of our classrooms. What positive policies and conversions can be pursued to redress these trends, to cultivate responsibility and integrity of behavior in our schools, and to mend the tattered fabric of community?

NOTES

1. David A. Hamberg, "Preparing for Life: The Critical Transition of Adolescence," from the *1986 Annual Report of the Carnegie Corporation* (New York: Carnegie Corp., 1987).

2. Carnegie Council on Adolescent Development, *Turning Points* (June 1989), p. 22. See also DHHS Publication No. (ADM) 89–1602, *Illicit Drug Use, Smoking and Drinking by America's High School Students, College Students, and Young Adults, 1975–1987* (Washington, D.C.: Government Printing Office, 1989).

3. *Newsweek,* March 21, 1988, p. 29.

4. See David C. McClelland, ed., *Education for Values* (New York: Irvington Publishers, 1982), p. 9.

5. *Ethics: Easier Said Than Done* (published by the Josephson Institute for the Advancement of Ethics), 1, no.1, p. 55.

6. *Newsweek on Campus* (Supplement to *Newsweek*), April 1984, p. 21.

7. *Turning Points,* p. 25.

8. *Carnegie Quarterly* (vol. 31, Summer/Fall 1986), p. 2. See also *11 Million Teenagers: What Can Be Done About the Epidemic of*

Teenage Pregnancies (New York: Alan Guttmacher Institute, 1976).

9. Children's Defense Fund, *Black Families and Children* (Washington, D.C.: Children's Defense Fund, 1988), p. 12.

10. Howard Lowry, *The Mind's Adventure: Religions in Higher Education* (Philadelphia: Westminster Press, 1950), p. 41.

11. Charles Glenn, "Molding Citizens," in Richard Neuhaus, ed., *Democracy and the Renewal of Public Education* (Grand Rapids: Eerdmans, 1987), p. 39.

12. John Westerhoff, *McGuffey and His Readers* (Nashville: Abingdon, 1978), p. 14.

13. Ibid., p. 94.

14. See Christopher Lasch, *The Culture of Narcissism* (New York: Norton, 1978).

15. Children's Defense Fund, *A Call for Action to Make Our Nation Safe for Children* (Washington, D.C.: Children's Defense Fund, 1988), p. iv.

16. Kenneth Keniston and the Carnegie Council on Children, *All Our Children: The American Family Under Pressure* (New York: Harcourt Brace Jovanovich, 1977).

17. *Time,* March 25, 1987, p. 28.

18. See chap. 6, "The Ethics of Communication," in Waldo Beach, *The Wheel and the Cross: A Christian Response to the Technological Revolution* (Atlanta: John Knox Press, 1979); and McClelland, *Education for Values,* chap. 3.

19. National Commission on Excellence in Education, *A Nation at Risk* (Washington, D.C.: Government Printing Office, 1983). See also an article by Derek Bok, president of Harvard, in *Ethics, Easier Said Than Done* 1, no. 1, and chap. 9, "Education, Wisdom or Skills?" in Beach, *The Wheel and the Cross.*

20. *New York Times,* Sunday, January 3, 1988, Week in Review, p. 14.

21. *Habits of the Heart: Individualism and Commitment in American Life* (New York: Harper and Row, 1985).

Chapter 2

THE REMEDY OF THE CONSERVATIVE RELIGIOUS RIGHT

RESTORE THE "FAITH OF OUR FATHERS"

One answer to the quandaries discussed in Chapter 1 is voiced by those of strong religious conviction who speak from what is termed the "Religious Right." Conservatives in the literal sense of that term, members of this group want to "conserve" the religious and moral traditions of the past, which to their alarm are fast being abandoned. They claim that the breakdown of moral behavior in our schools is the inevitable consequence of the loss of the traditional religious tenets of faith upon which this nation was founded. These principles assured our moral health and civility until the cults of materialism, sensuality, and permissiveness infected America in this century. Therefore, the only remedy is to recover the "faith of our fathers" and to instill this faith in the hearts and minds of our children.

This persuasion is not new. It has been heard again and again in our political rhetoric. George Washington's Farewell Address warned that "Religion and experience both forbid us to expect that national morality can prevail in exclusion of religious principle." The same note is repeated in presidential inaugural addresses. As former President Ronald Reagan addressed an evangelical prayer breakfast in 1984: "The truth is, politics and morality are inseparable. And as morality's foundation is religion, religion and politics are necessarily related. . . . If we ever forget that we're one nation under God, then we will be a nation gone under."[1]

The relation of religious faith to morality is an issue far more complex than can be treated adequately here. What is meant by "religious faith"? Which religion? Christianity,

Judaism, Buddhism, Islam? Is the "Humanist Manifesto" a statement of a religious creed?

In the last half century the Supreme Court has been ambiguous in its interpretation of the First Amendment: "Congress shall make no law respecting an establishment of religion, or prohibiting the free exercise thereof." On church-state decisions, it has sometimes favored the "free exercise" clause, allowing the expression of religion in schools. For example, a decision handed down in May 1990 permits voluntary Bible study clubs to meet in public schools. At other times it has favored the "establishment" clause, prohibiting the expression of religion.[2] The master metaphor in common parlance is the "wall of separation" between church and state. Under the spell of that metaphor, expressions of religious faith have been generally excluded from public education.

The evangelical Religious Right, however, is not at all equivocal. The true religion that must be restored to all our schools, public and private, is Christianity. Piety and reverence before God revealed in Christ are required to cultivate a moral and responsible conscience and to recover traditional "family values." This faith is consummately set forth in the Bible. Therefore the only way to restore decency and decorum in the classroom is by Bible study and public prayer, to cultivate a spirit of reverence, for "the fear of the Lord is the beginning of wisdom" (Ps. 111:10). One way to assure right behavior is by strict discipline. Corporal punishment, justified on biblical grounds (Prov. 13:24), was common practice in Puritan homes and schools. "Spare the rod and spoil the child." So, strict discipline should be again practiced.

This serious conviction about the religious core of education, we should note, is by no means confined to evangelical Protestants of the Religious Right. There are many parents of strong religious faith, Roman Catholic, Episcopal, Presbyterian, Friends, Mennonite, who are disillusioned by the "secular" and morally anomic atmosphere of public schools, where devotional exercises and religious indoctrination are ruled out of bounds by some Supreme Court rulings on the First Amendment. This is one of the reasons why these parents enroll their children in private schools where religion is made an essential part of the life of the school.

Many factors have been at play in the development of private education at every level. The right of parents to send their children to private schools of their choice, or even to have schooling at home, at all levels, as long as certain educational criteria are met, has long been an established right protected by law. Yet the motives behind the exercise of this right, to opt out of public school programs, are certainly morally mixed. Since *Brown v. Board of Education,* which required racial integration in the public schools, the growth of the so-called Christian Academies, especially in the South, represents in part a white flight from racial integration. This has tended to decrease the day-by-day contacts between white and Black children and their families. To be sure, many private schools, North and South, are attempting to increase the enrollment of students of minority ethnic groups. But by and large these schools are white, since relatively few Black families can afford to enroll their children in them. Consequently there is almost always a white homogeneity in a private school that is not present in a public school. American public policy is committed to providing *all* children with an equal opportunity for education, but that mandate applies only to the public school system; private schools are generally free to be selective in their admissions. It is in the public schools, then, that this heterogeneous mixture of colors, religious beliefs, cultural backgrounds, and abilities prevails and ideally fosters a crucial aspect of moral education of our youth: that is, a spirit of respect for ethnic and racial variety.

Since the parents who send their children to private schools are obliged to pay tuition and also to pay regular taxes to support existing public schools, this double load has prompted a movement, backed by many conservative officials in the administration, to provide tuition vouchers, to ease what seems an unjust burden. Furthermore, the white flight in suburbia to private schools, where the quality of educational standards is generally high, has served to lower the quality of education in the public schools of the inner city.

A NORMATIVE ASSESSMENT OF THE CONSERVATIVE CRUSADE

How should one fairly measure by ethical criteria this new wave of religious conservatism in its motives and practices? The scorecard of merits and faults is mixed. Positively, one may say that the education of character and the nurture of conscience in social responsibility is indeed as important in education as schooling in the basic skills. To instill a sense of integrity, trust, accountability, caring, should be an essential part of the process of maturation, instead of nurturing an anomic, normless lifestyle where the pursuit of sensual pleasure, power, and material gain has replaced the traditional values of our Judeo-Christian heritage. Certain fixed laws of human interaction are the sinews of a civil society. In a recent commencement address at a major university, Ted Koppel, the TV anchorman, put it bluntly: "What Moses brought down from Mount Sinai were not the Ten Suggestions. They are the Ten Commandments. . . . They codify in a handful of words acceptable human behavior, not just for then or now but for all time." In 1978, Tennessee passed a law requiring the posting of the Ten Commandments in each public school classroom, although each display added a disclaimer: "The secular application of the Ten Commandments is clearly seen . . . as the fundamental legal code of Western Civilization and the common law of the United States."

Since 1971, in *Lemon v. Kurtzman,* the Supreme Court has applied a three-pronged test to judge the constitutionality of policies and practices regarding religion in public schools: "the statute must have a secular legislative purpose," it must have a "primary effect that neither advances nor inhibits religion," and its administration must avoid "excessive governmental entanglement with religion."[3] So in 1980 the Court banned this policy in

23

Tennessee schools on the grounds that it was *not* secular in purpose.

But religious conservatives are quick to point out that the "neutrality" policy as to the treatment of religion set in recent Supreme Court decisions is not really neutral in effect. When the Court says that in a statute concerning the treatment of religion in public schooling "its principal or primary effect must be one that neither advances nor inhibits religion," the general practice is for teachers to avoid dealing with religion entirely. Consequently, students get the impression that religious faiths and practices are insignificant and irrelevant. The "primary effect," then, is not a neutral but a negative one.[4]

It is interesting to note that this conviction is shared by educators of liberal persuasion. In North Carolina a state committee of the board of education reported that this "neutrality" mandated by the Supreme Court has led to a serious neglect of the study of religion in the curricula of public schools in history, social sciences, and literature. Students are bleakly illiterate about the crucial role religion has played in the cultures of the world. People for the American Way, a staunch opponent of the Christian evangelical movement's effort to propagate the Christian gospel among our children, nonetheless acknowledges that teaching *about* religion—and that means world religions—is much needed.[5]

On the other side of the scorecard, however, many serious faults appear in the crusade of the evangelical Religious Right. A 30-second prayer at the beginning of the school day, or even a mandated moment of silent meditation, can hardly be said to "bring God back into the public schools," or to assure moral propriety in behavior for the rest of the day in the classroom or at recess in the school yard. Opponents of the school prayer rightly claim that such a practice trivializes what should be a serious devotional attitude.[6]

Another dangerous aspect of the moral crusade of the conservative Right and the Fundamentalists lies in their campaign to censor textbooks and to ban books that they are

24

convinced would corrupt the minds and the morality of children. In early 1988, a federal court in Florida upheld the removal of books by Chaucer and Aristophanes from a high school humanities class, according to an ACLU newsletter. On one occasion a group of devout parents demanded that school boards remove such books as *Catcher in the Rye, The Wizard of Oz, Huckleberry Finn, The Diary of Anne Frank,* and *The Grapes of Wrath.* The parents took their case to court, arguing that their religious rights were violated, since these books promote such "anti-Christian themes as evolution, feminism, and pacifism." John Steinbeck's *Of Mice and Men* was the most frequently protested book, because its pages are spiced with profanity.[7] A conservative lobby group, the Eagle Forum, headed by Phyllis Schlafly, opposed the use of popular novels of Judy Blume because of their references to sexual encounters. "Schools should teach sexual abstinence before marriage. If you tell them [students] about contraception you're condoning something contrary to religion and morality."[8] Fortunately, the Supreme Court has recently overruled a lower court decision that upheld the book-banning rights of the parents. After all, education authorities and experts should determine the content of the curriculum.

Another serious flaw in this attempt to recover the faith of our fathers and to bring God back into public schools derives from its tight biblicism. The inerrantist Fundamentalist view of the Bible, from Genesis through Revelations, as absolutely literally true in a historic and scientific sense as well as in its spiritual sense, and therefore not subject to critical interpretation, runs sharply counter to a basic principle of education.

In recent decades a storm of controversy has arisen between the advocates of so-called "scientific creationism" and the Darwinian theory of evolution. Some devout parents have claimed that scientific creationism should be given equal time with the Darwinian evolutionary theory in high school biology courses. The furies of this storm cloud have swept into classrooms and school boards. A high school teacher teaching a course in the

Bible as literature may be confronted with a protest of some parents when she explains that Genesis 1 is a mythological account of creation, not a scientific account. If students are told that the world was created in seven days, this runs counter to what they are studying in biology, where the gradual evolution of the human species over millions of years is explained and documented by hard evidence. The whole controversy has been carried through the court system. A major decision of Judge William Overton in 1982 overturned an Arkansas lower court ruling that allowed "balanced treatment" of the biblical and the Darwinian views.[9] Judge Overton ruled that "creation science is not science," but a disguised version of a particular religious view, and therefore not allowable. But the Fundamentalists stick to their position. They fail to see that the "mythology" of the Bible may not be literally true but authentic truth expressed in poetic, graphic imagery rather than in the empirical language of fact. "He walks on the wings of the wind, and makes the clouds his chariots," says the Psalmist. Here is a magnificent expression of God's power, but God is not walking "up there" or riding on a chariot. This whole controversy remains blocked, a stalemate, a misplaced debate.[10]

The strict biblicism of the conservative Religious Right leads it into another serious pitfall, in its claim that the Bible should be a rule book for all ethical choices. The precepts of the Decalogue, the Sermon on the Mount, or the Pauline Epistles do indeed set the basic norms of the good life. But when it comes to the particular tight dilemmas of choice the teenager faces in the course of a day, the Bible is not of practical help as a rule book. For example, a conservative magazine, *Christian Parenting,* claims that God's Word provides practical guidance in dealing with such problems as "bedwetting, sibling rivalry, reading/learning disabilities, peer pressure." Such claims are outlandish. "Bedwetting" is not listed in any biblical concordance.

Finally, the cause of the conservative Religious Right is faulted by a sociological fact: the ethnic and religious pluralism of the American population represented by the mixture of students now enrolled in public schools. America is no longer a pan-Protestant society. In the typical inner-city school one may likely find children from Jewish, Black Muslim, Hispanic, Hindu, and Buddhist families, along with a variety of Protestants and Roman Catholics. And many children are from families with no religious affiliation at all. To impose a narrow fundamentalist evangelical Protestant version of the Christian faith as the only true religion, the only foundation on which to build character, violates the religious and legal rights of all these differing groups. Should Michael Cohen, a Jewish eighth grader, be told by his Baptist teacher, an ardent "born-again" Christian, that unless one is "saved" by Christ, he or she will be consigned to an after-life in hell? That would be not only illegal, clashing with the disestablishment clause of the First Amendment, but cruel and immoral. There are, to be sure, many moral norms shared by Christians and non-Christians. But the imposition of one variant of the Christian faith as the only authentic version in the midst of the pluralism of our current society is a violation of the basic principle of religious freedom and rights. Furthermore, it also encourages a narrow and parochial view of religion in the minds of students. As a matter of fact, current studies have not shown any direct correlation of religious or church affiliation with moral sensitivity and responsible conduct.[11]

On balance, then, we are led to conclude that the proposed remedies of the Religious Right for the ethical problems in public education, to cultivate responsible conscience and conduct among our school children, however sincerely and devoutly intended, are not ethically right, legally proper, or practically feasible. We must look in another direction for guidance.

NOTES

1. See Waldo Beach, ed., *Church, State and Education* Chapel Hill: University of North Carolina Press, 1985), pp. 8ff. Senator Jesse Helms of North Carolina once phrased his conviction thus: "I believe in freedom of religion, but not freedom from religion."

27

2. See Philip Kurland, *Religion and the Law* (Chicago; University of Chicago Press, 1961); Joseph Tussman, ed., *The Supreme Court on Church and State* (New York: Oxford University Press, 1961); John Semonche, ed., *Religion and Law In American History* (Chapel Hill: University of North Carolina Press, 1985); Mark deWolfe Howe, *The Garden and the Wilderness: Religion and Government in American Constitutional History* (Chicago: University of Chicago Press, 1965).

3. See *Lemon v. Kurtzman* (403 U.S. 602, 1971) and *Walz v. Tax Commission* (397 U.S. 664, 1970). Also Charles Haynes, *Religious Freedom in America: A Teacher's Guide* (Silver Spring, Md.: Americans United Research Foundation, 1986).

4. See James Hitchcock, "Disentangling the Secular Humanism Debate," in Carl Horn, ed., *Whose Values: The Battle for Morality in Pluralistic America* (Ann Arbor: University of Michigan Press, 1985). See also U.S. Department of Education, "Equity in Value Education: Religion in American Textbooks: A Review of the Literature," (Washington, D.C.: Government Printing Office, 1985); and Paul Vitz, "A Study of Religious and Traditional Values in Public School Textbooks," in Richard Neuhaus, ed., *Democracy and the Renewal of Public Education* (Grand Rapids: Eerdmans, 1987).

5. People for the American Way, *Attacks on the Freedom to Learn* (1988), as reported in the *New York Times,* Sept. 1, 1988.

6. See Beach, *Church, State,* pp. 22–28.

7. See "The Battle of the Books," in *Forum: Newsletter for the People for the American Way,* Spring 1990.

8. Phyllis Schlafly, *Child Abuse in the Classroom* (Alton, Ill.: Pere Marquette Press, 1984). Ms. Schlafly would apply a litmus test of questions whereby parents are to judge the quality of their children's education. Here are two of the many questions put: "Does it lead the child to believe that there are no absolute moral standards, but that the morality of an act depends on the situation? . . . Does it affirmatively teach the ideology of secular humanism or that all religions are equally valid?" (p. 436). If your answer is yes, you should protest to the school board.

9. *McLean v. The Arkansas Board of Education* (D. Ark. 1982).

10. See Roland Frye, ed., *Is God a Creationist? The Religious Case Against Creation-Science* (New York: Scribners, 1983).

11. Gary L. Sapp, "Moral Judgment and Religious Orientation," in Gary Sapp, ed., *Handbook of Moral Development* (Birmingham: Religious Education Press, 1986).

Chapter 3

TWO SECULAR PROGRAMS
OF MORAL EDUCATION

An entirely different approach to moral education from that of the conservative Religious Right is that advanced by professional theorists of education and child psychologists. In the last two or three decades, a vast amount of literature has appeared. It includes guidelines and handbooks for teachers and guidance counselors to assist students in cultivating "habits of the heart" and habits of conduct that are appropriate to their age level and maturity. While these professional educators are aware of the serious moral deterioration of common life in our public schools, they share the strong conviction that the best remedy for these problems is not to try to restore Protestant piety and reverence as the only valid foundation of responsible behavior. Rather, their premises are more humanistic and secular. We shall consider in brief two such approaches: the values clarification school of thought and the cognitive-development theories. Then follows a critical assessment of the merits and faults of each approach.

Values Clarification

Values and Teaching by Louis Raths, Merrill Harmon, and Sidney Simon[1] gave impetus to a movement widely used in the 60s known as values clarification. The main intent of this program is for teachers to assist pupils, at whatever age or stage of moral development, to sort out the values at stake in their decisions, to clarify the values they prize, to consider alternative consequences of one option or another, to affirm what they prize and cherish, and to act upon their cherished values in a consistent manner. In all of this guidance, it is claimed, the teacher should not "zap" the pupil with an imperial rule. No disciple of the VC method should mandate morality, saying, "This is the right way to behave. That is the wrong way to behave." Indoctrination is the worst form of moral education, for it imposes upon the child some bag of rules that he or she may not understand or accept and may very likely resist. The most deadly pedagogical sin is moral imperialism. As Simon and his colleagues affirmed, "In areas involving aspirations, purposes, attitudes, interests, beliefs, etc., we [as teachers] may raise questions, but we cannot 'lay down the law' about what a child's values should be. By definition and by social right, then, values are personal things."[2]

The cardinal pedagogical virtue of this way of helping students come to their own value persuasions is neutrality. "The clarifying response avoids moralizing, criticizing, giving values, or evaluating. The adult excludes all hints of 'good' or 'right' or 'acceptable,' or any of their opposites in such responses."[3] Presumably by this gentle strategy of permissive question-raising a pupil may come to recognize that some values such as courtesy, diligence, truth-telling, fair play and justice are preferable to rudeness, sloth, lying, stealing, and the like.

There may be some merits in the VC method of moral education, such as its avoidance of a harsh imposition of a strict moral code that elicits only a response of surly compliance or sly deviation from the rules. But on closer look the VC method by and large proves a flimsy and vulnerable way of cultivating sensitive consciences and responsible conduct. It carries the Socratic method to an absurd extreme. It commits what philosophers call the "naturalistic fallacy," by failing to distinguish between "is" and "ought." The values a student prizes may not be the ones he or she *ought* to prize.

For example, imagine the following scenario. A teacher happens to come upon an eighth grader fumbling in another student's locker in the hallway:

T. Hello, Paul. Say, what are you doing there?
S. Well . . . uh . . . I'm getting some money to buy sandwiches for lunch.

31

T. Is it yours?

S. Sure . . . Well, no, I forgot to bring my own today. I mean, my mother didn't have any cash to give me.

T. Whose locker are you in? Isn't that Priscilla's?

S. Yeah, I guess so.

T. Thanks for being honest. But why? Don't you think she'll be angry with you?

S. Maybe. But I've got to get some money for lunch. I'm hungry.

T. So you value a dollar more than your friendship with Priscilla. What would she think of that? What if everybody who needed money stole somebody else's? OK, Paul, you think about it, will you? See you later.

If the matter were closed with this exchange in the hall, it is not likely that Paul would be educated in moral concern or in respect for persons and property, nor would the teacher be fulfilling her responsibility to him. A more conscientious followup of this dialogue would be for the teacher to refer the incident to the principal's office, or to the guidance counselor, for disciplinary measures to be taken, for Priscilla's money to be returned, and perhaps for the parents to be informed of the incident.

Critics are quick to point out that the proponents of VC are not in fact really as value-neutral as their first principles claim. The advocates of the VC method acknowledge, quite inconsistently with their credo, that some kinds of conduct—"profane language, obscene behavior, filth, and dirtiness"—may not be tolerated.[4]

A leading champion of VC, Sidney Simon, on the one hand opposes all "indoctrination" of moral values, but on the other actually takes very strong explicit moral stands against materialism, racism, and war:

How can we get men and women to take on some larger share of their personal responsibility for the rampant racism in our nation? Or for allowing a senseless war to continue indefinitely? When will educators make a contribution toward helping people examine the headlong pursuit towards accumulating more and more material possessions and enjoying them less?[5]

The critics of VC, both teachers in schools and in the university departments of education, point out another basic weakness of this method. It runs deeper than the inconsistency between its nonjudgmental value-neutrality and some strong moral judgments we have alluded to. It is the basic moral *anomie* or *normlessness,* a complete relativism that makes matters of ethical right and wrong purely a matter of individual preference. This is not far from "If it feels good, do it." On the larger question of the meta-ethical foundations of value or of social accountability it is silent. In dealing with such rampant problems as drug addiction or teenage sexual promiscuity and the high rate of pregnancies among teenage girls, is the teacher or counselor limited by VC to having students "clarify" their actions by acknowledging that "Everybody's doing it," or "I just wanted to get high"?

Moreover, as another critic points out, VC fails to provide guidance in situations of moral collision that constitute our daily fare, when one prized or "cherished" value collides with another and one has "to rob Peter to pay Paul."[6] For example, parental approval often conflicts with peer-group pressure when it comes to choosing some forms of fun. The value of getting high grades sometimes collides with the value of integrity and accountability in writing exams or papers. Even if one has clarified the dilemma, VC in itself offers no moral guidance as to which value is to be sacrificed and which preferred. In this morass of normlessness the frequent wild and chaotic behavior of young people betrays a hidden desperation for boundaries and guidelines for their lives.

Furthermore, the success of the VC method would seem to require a great deal of one-on-one teacher-student dialogue; each teacher would need to be sensitive to the vast range of individual differences among his or her students. It is difficult to imagine how to bring this off when dealing with a class of 30 or more pupils, with whom one may have only an hour's contact in the school day. To be sure, this problem besets any program of moral education.

In sum, despite its immediate appeal and glamor as a protest against some of the inhumane aspects of schooling in Puritan days when moral rules were clear and their violations punished severely, the VC approach fails to provide the needed cure for our moral malaise. It is no surprise that it has fallen out of fashion.

THE COGNITIVE-DEVELOPMENT PRESCRIPTION

A more thorough and substantial theory of moral education is the "cognitive-development" view, associated especially with the name of Lawrence Kohlberg, whose research and writings in the 1970s have come into wide usage. Much indebted to the psychological theories of Jean Piaget and reflecting also the premises of John Dewey's theory of education, Kohlberg proposed a structural theory of stages of moral development.

Carefully and extensively tested by longitudinal studies of students of every age and many different cultures, Kohlberg's hypothesis is that there are clearly differentiated moral stages of development that are universal and follow an "invariant sequence" from lower to higher. Each has two substages within it. Kohlberg defines the stages as follows:

I. *Preconventional Level.* Here the child's response to what is called "good or bad" is in terms of "the physical or hedonistic consequences of action."

Stage 1. Punishment-and-obedience orientation. The rightness or wrongness of actions is determined simply by whether they will be rewarded or punished.

Stage 2. The instrumental-relativist orientation. At this stage "right action consists of that which instrumentally satisfies one's own needs and occasionally the needs of others," but "the reciprocity is interpreted as a pragmatic matter of 'you scratch my back and I'll scratch yours.'"

II. *Conventional Level.* Here the morality of an action is defined by "maintaining the expectations of the individual's family, group, or nation."

Stage 3. "The interpersonal concordance or 'good boy-nice girl' orientation." Good behavior is what conforms to the group's standard; bad behavior is what does not conform."

Stage 4. "The law and order" orientation. Morality at this stage is understood in terms of obedience to authority and maintaining the social order.

III. *Postconventional Level.* Autonomous or principled levels. Here the worth of moral values is intrinsic and may be defined apart from the authority of persons who enforce or require behavior in keeping with them.

Stage 5. The social contract-legalistic orientation. Here right action is determined by adherence to general individual rights.

Stage 6. The universal ethical principle orientation. "Right is defined by the decision of conscience in accord with self-chosen ethical principles appealing to logical comprehensiveness, universality, and consistency. Such principles are those of justice, reciprocity, and equality of rights, and respect for the worth of individual persons. At this highest stage of moral maturity a person acts in accord with the dictates of conscience, in allegiance to the principle of justice, even if this conviction should run counter to the prevailing tide of popular opinion."[7]

Obviously Kohlberg's theory is a more psychologically sophisticated and philosophically grounded theory of moral education than the VC method. The shades of difference between his six stages of moral development are subtle indeed, although one could readily see the distance between Stage 1 and

Stage 6. Kohlberg does not propose his theory as a quick-fix formula for the development of conscience or character. He acknowledges that children as well as adults, for that matter, in the basic motivation for decisions and actions, at best rarely move beyond stages 3 or 4. Obedience to conscience, as a "principle within" in allegiance to universal norms of justice is not the usual guideline for the majority of people.

Imagine this implausible scenario:

> Mom and Dad are setting off for an evening out and the sitter, Robbie, has just arrived to monitor their eight-year-old while they are gone.
> Dad: Johnny, we'll be back kind of late. Now be good while we're out, OK?
> Johnny: Dad, before you go could you define what constitutes the essence of "goodness"?

Even if Dad were versed in the cognitive-development theory of Kohlberg, he would be hard put to give a ready and coherent answer. It is unlikely that he would quote Kant's categorical imperative. He'd simply say, "Do what Robbie tells you to do. If you don't, we won't let you go to the Cub Scout outing tomorrow." (Kohlberg would interpret this exchange to mean that both Johnny and his father are at Stage 1 of moral development.)

It is significant that there is a strong normative element in Kohlberg's presumably descriptive analysis. That is to say, while he concentrates on the psychological description of the factors that motivate children and adolescents at these various stages, his normative conclusion is that moral maturity in the educational process is realized when persons move on their own from lower to higher stages, as aided by others, from the "carrot-stick" motivations to the conscientious allegiance to principles of justice, equality, and regard for the worth of persons. His theory is *not* value-neutral, for he affirms that the principled stages of moral reasoning are morally better stages than the lower ones.[8]

But Kohlberg is certainly realistic in acknowledging that the eighth grader in the scenario mentioned earlier would be motivated not to steal money from Priscilla's locker more out of fear of punishment if caught than out of a comprehension of the basic principle of justice and respect for persons. Kohlberg is also impressive in his recognition that the "hidden curriculum" of the school, "the crowds, the praise, and the power" (a phrase from Emile Durkheim), influences moral development even more than the "visible" curriculum of the textbook and the content of courses. The morale of the school in the quality of interpersonal relations among teachers, pupils, administrators, athletic coaches, and counselors is profoundly important in the education of conscience. This matter of the hidden curriculum will be discussed in Chapter 5.

Both secular and religious critics have raised serious questions about Kohlberg's cognitive-development theory, however. While it is convincing in a descriptive sense, certain flaws appear when we assess it in a normative sense.

The basic problem is in its overemphasis on the *cognitive* aspect of moral development. A perennial issue in all ethical theories is the dialectic of the cognitive versus the affective sides of moral decision or, to use terms of an older vintage, the mind versus the heart or the will. Do ethical actions flow from the mind's clear analysis of the values in a tight dilemma of choice, or from the heart's desire? Kohlberg acknowledges that "will, then, is an important factor in moral behavior, but it is not distinctively moral; it becomes moral only when informed by mature moral judgment."[9] This cognitive stress on the reasoning aspect of moral decision neglects one classical element especially strong in the Judeo-Christian heritage: the loves of the heart. As St. Augustine put it centuries ago, "When there is a question as to whether a man is good, one does not ask what he believes, or what he hopes, but what he loves."[10] In Kohlberg's stress on the cognitive aspect of moral growth, inadequate attention is given to the voluntaristic springs of moral decision, the desires of the heart

37

that may run counter to what the mind discerns. As Derek Bok has put it, "Reasoning alone will not suffice to build character."[11]

The second problem—the moral norms of justice, reciprocity and equality of rights and the respect for persons, which guide the conscience of those at the highest stage, do not in themselves assist at the moral nexus of choice where these rights are in collision. The Kantian principle of justice does not assist my choice between the needs of some persons as they conflict with the needs of others. Take, for instance, the problem of rights and wrongs of affirmative action, now currently litigated in our courts, where one person's conscience may choose to grant unequal advantages to minorities in order to redress the imbalance of past injustices of racial discrimination, while another person conscientiously insists on a color-blind equality. Or do the needs of the starving people in Haiti or Zaire lay as compelling a claim on my conscience as those of the impoverished people in Harlem or rural Appalachia? The constituents of the norm of justice, at this principled level, Kohlberg affirms, "are, first, the maximum liberty compatible with the like liberty of others, and, second, no inequalities of goods and respect which are not to the benefit of all, including the least advantaged."[12] But when one is forced to choose within a moral economy of scarcity, where the benefit of some must be sacrificed to the benefit of others, such a normative principle of justice is of limited use.

A third critique of Kohlberg's view is heard from those who speak from the Judeo-Christian religious tradition. They would claim that Kohlberg, as a child of the Enlightenment, has a view of human nature that is rationalistic and optimistic about the human potential to discern the moral good and to conduct behavior accordingly. His cognitive approach does not reckon with the phenomenon presumed in Judeo-Christian thought of *rationalization*—that is, the capacity of human nature to disguise morally wrong motives with good reasons, or "to make the worse appear the better reason." In brief, as one critic put it, "he does not take human sinfulness seriously. . . . Human sinfulness continually distorts our reason, our role-taking, our social perspectives, and our ego-development."[13] Here the will uses the mind to cover its wrongs with excuses and claims to innocence. Any parent or teacher can attest to this phenomenon. When a child or adolescent engages in wrongdoing and is challenged, the immediate response is a claim to innocence and the transfer of fault to someone or something else. The mind becomes an excuse-making machine.

In the classical Judeo-Christian tradition of moral theology, much attention is given to the nature of conscience, as the inner principle that determines choice and where rightly turned leads to right behavior. However, much attention is also given to the troubled or guilty or "accusing" conscience, where the inner self comes to acknowledge that it has acted in violation of the moral norms the self knows or at least has professed in principle. Guilt, remorse, contrition, repentance, forgiveness—these traditional categories of moral theology—are lacking in Kohlberg's descriptive and normative analysis of cognitive moral development. Yet from a religious perspective, conscience, whether guilty or "easy," is a concept essential to the true understanding of growth to responsible moral maturity.

Finally, a deficiency in Kohlberg's theory of moral education is his lack of attention to the "meta-ethical" bases of the moral norms of justice, equality, and consideration of the worth of persons. From a religious point of view, in the final analysis the highest moral norms are not autonomous, but are theonomous, that is, grounded in a transcendent will of God, to whom the conscience is ultimately accountable. In his later writings, Kolhberg came to acknowledge the vital part religious faith may play in moral maturation.[14] But as one of his critics points out, "In Kohlberg, religion consists mainly of a person's conception of the ultimate nature of reality. Religion is not concerned with a transcendent being quite other in nature from ourselves, mostly hidden, and ultimately an unfathomable but nonetheless active mystery. . . . Religious faith and belief have been collapsed here into human psychological structures."[15] For

Kohlberg it would seem that traditional religious principles, symbols, rituals, practices of prayer and worship—quite apart from the question of their legality in public schools—have no place in nurturing consciences or cultivating right conduct. Reverence is no longer the beginning of wisdom. These practices that were followed in the common schools of the nineteenth century, such as required chapel, community rituals of recognition, and shared celebrations, were directed to the hearts of those participating. They inspired a certain morale as important for moral nurture as the cognitive learning exercises. These affective factors in public education are rarely found today.

There is much psychological wisdom in Kohlberg's cognitive-development theory. And his view accords implicitly with the best of our various religious traditions, that the moral norms of justice and reciprocity have an ontological base and are not simply of human contrivance. Yet in his failure to deal with the affective or volitional aspects of morality and with human sin, the cognitive development theory falls short.[16]

NOTES

1. *Values and Teaching* (Columbus, Ohio: Charles Merrill, 1966). See also Simon et al. *Values Clarification: A Handbook of Practical Strategies for Teachers and Students* (New York: Hart, 1972); and Robert T. Hall and John U. Davis, *Moral Education in Theory and Practice* (Buffalo: Prometheus Books, 1975).

2. *Values and Teaching*, p. 37.

3. Ibid., p. 53.

4. Ibid., p. 134, 144-45.

5. David Purpel and Kevin Ryan, eds., *Moral Education: It Comes with the Territory* (Berkeley: McCutchan Publishing, 1976), p. 83.

6. Ibid., p. 155.

7. Kohlberg defines and elaborates on these stages of moral development at many points in his numerous writings. This summary is taken from Peter Scharf, ed., *Readings in Moral*

Education (Minneapolis: Winston Press, 1978), pp. 50, 51, and 308 (Appendix). The same is to be found in Purpel and Ryan, *Moral Education,* pp. 215-16.

8. Purpel and Ryan, *Moral Education,* p. 182.

9. Ibid., p. 181.

10. *Enchiridion,* chap. 117.

11. See Derek Bok, *Universities and the Future of America* (Durham: Duke University Press, 1990), chaps. 3, 4.

12. Purpel and Ryan, *Moral Education* p. 183. This reflects also the view of John Rawls: *A Theory of Justice* (Cambridge, Mass.: Harvard University Press, 1971).

13. Craig Dykstra, "What Are People Like: An Alternative to Kohlberg's View," in Donald Joy, ed., *Moral Development Foundations: Judeo-Christian Alternatives to Piaget/Kohlberg* (Nashville: Abingdon Press, 1983), p. 153, 155. See also Dykstra's *Vision and Character* (Ramsey, N.J.: Paulist Press, 1981).

14. See Lawrence Kohlberg, "Education, Moral Development, and Faith," in *Journal of Moral Education* (1974).

15. Dykstra, *Vision and Character,* p. 26.

16. See chaps. 18 (R. S. Peters) and 19 (Jack Fraenkel) in Purpel and Ryan, *Moral Education.* Also Carol Gilligan, *In a Different Voice: Psychological Theory in Women's Development* (Cambridge: Harvard University Press, 1982), pp. 18, 20. Gilligan criticizes Kohlberg's male chauvinism and his failure to appreciate the feminine perspective on ethics, one of caring and compassion.

Chapter 4

A PREFERABLE STRATEGY OF MORAL EDUCATION

The two preceding chapters reviewed sharply different approaches to moral education—the view of the conservative Religious Right and the theories of values clarification and Kohlberg's cognitive-development. Although both approaches have merit in their serious attention to the importance of nurturing the consciences of students in public schools, both prove to be deficient—the former for its narrow religious dogmatism, the latter for their preoccupation with descriptive and cognitive analyses and their failure to deal with the normative and volitional or affective aspects of moral education. This critique leads us to chart a course that steers between the two views, which may provide a better and more realistic guideline for ethical education.

If we are correct that the cultivation of conscience, moral responsibility, and right conduct is indeed one of the central aims of all education, public or private, a definition of the meaning of "conscience" is needed. Obviously conscience is not some automated green-light red-light mechanism that flashes "yes-go" or "no-stop" at the crossroads of a moral choice. It would be naive to define conscience in such simplistic terms—as it would be of little avail for a parent to counsel a teenager, off for her first coed weekend party at the beach, "Let your conscience be your guide."[1]

From the past heritage of moral philosophy and theology, as well as from more recent psychology, we learn that a person's conscience at whatever age is a syndrome of attitudes: an inner sense of accountability to other persons, an allegiance to the values one prizes as of supreme worth, from which follow actions consistent with those values, where one's action is "as good as one's word." This corresponds to Kohlberg's Stage 6 of moral development: "principled action." The inner integrity, thus defined, and conduct consistent with that integrity, give the person an "easy" or "good" conscience. However, when the individual's actions run counter to this inner principle, and he/she is haunted in hindsight by this disparity, the conscience becomes a "guilty" or "accusing" conscience, to use terms common in moral theology.[2]

There are several diverse traditions concerning the basis of conscience. The Judeo-Christian heritage regards conscience as having a transcendent source, "the voice of God" speaking in the inner self. Roman Catholic moral theology defines it as *synderesis,* the faculty that discerns the moral mandates of God's will, and *conscientia,* the application of these to particular decisions. Protestant theologians, especially those of the Calvinistic tradition, wrote many treatises on cases of conscience, dealing both with its positive and negative aspects. In *Paradise Lost,* John Milton's Creator pronounced:

And I will place within them as a guide
My umpire conscience, which, if they will hear,
Light after Light well used they shall attain
And to the end persisting safe arrive.

Another Puritan put it thus: "Conscience is of a divine nature and is a thing placed of God in the middest between Him and man, as an arbitrator to give sentence and to pronounce either with man or against man unto God."[3]

In our own day, the term *conscience* has been largely secularized, cleared of any theological referent. When one speaks of a person as "conscientious," it usually means diligent, honest, reliable, trustworthy. The matrix in which conscience is here defined is purely secular and social, having to do with one's relationship with peers or authorities. It has no transcendent divine source.

Kohlberg's cognitive-development theory is a good example. In one way, it provides a valuable corrective to the older

Christian tradition about the nature of conscience. Obviously we are not born with any "moral voice within," but our consciences are nurtured gradually by our lives at home and at school, through something like the stages that Kohlberg describes. Or they may be wrongly educated into an allegiance to false values.

Whether conscience is understood as monitored by a Divine Eye, as in traditional Christian terms, or simply nurtured and monitored by social controls, it is not simply a "principle within." One's outer conduct is a reflection of one's inner moral convictions. To be sure, often there is a wide disparity between conscience and behavior. To use St. Paul's words, "For I do not do the good I want, but the evil I do not want is what I do" (Romans 7:19).[4] It is this contradiction between inner moral persuasion and outer behavior that makes for a troubled or guilty conscience.

A major problem encountered in this interpretation of the schooling of consciences is the fact that moral choices for children and for adults as well are never posed as options between a clear good and a clear bad. The moral dilemmas daily confronted are options between two competing goods, where, as discussed above, one has to sacrifice on one to serve another, or where the choice may be to decide between the lesser of two evils. Values collide for any teacher or student many times a day. For a teacher, the virtue of disciplining a pupil with an "F" for failing to hand in a written paper on time, which might lead him or her to "shape up" on next week's assignment, contends with the merit of a sympathetic forgiveness that might induce better performance. Or where the school has an honor code, a student's conscience is torn between the merit of reporting an offense of a peer and the loyalty to that friend which might be cut if the student "squealed" on him or her. Or to get a high grade a student may sacrifice honesty to plagiarize material without acknowledgment. Here the goal of achievement competes with the principle of integrity. Or should the high school basketball coach bar the best player from the final tournament play-off game because of suspicion that the player has been using drugs and might test positive, even though without that player the team will probably lose? And the player faces the choice between the kicks of getting high at a party with the rest of the team members versus the risk of not being allowed to play. These are but a few examples of the value conflicts that arise daily in the hallways and classrooms of any school.

One college president addressing an entering freshman class spoke about the moral purposes of education in this way: "to make judgments between right and wrong, good and evil, just and unjust: to make the even harder choices between right and right, or, as is more often the case, between the mostly right and the partly right."[5]

ETHICAL EDUCATION IN THE VISIBLE CURRICULUM

Moral education occurs both through the prescribed curriculum of the schools—the study in health and natural sciences, in social sciences and history, in literature and the arts—and also within the "hidden" curriculum, that is, in the spirit and quality of the interpersonal relations of teachers, students, administrators, counselors, and athletic coaches, creating a certain morale. The hidden curriculum is just as crucial in forming character as is the visible curriculum.

Instruction and learning in the standard curriculum create a process that conveys more than facts. Moral issues also permeate the subjects studied, all the way from the classics of English literature to ecology in the earth science course.

Health Sciences and Hygiene

One part of the program of studies that affects student behavior most directly is the area of health sciences and hygiene. A subject of great concern currently is that of sex education.[6] As pointed out in Chapter 1, sexual activity, including intercourse, is an increasing common practice. Therefore, an important part of a health science course, even in the primary and middle school, should focus openly on the *facts* of sexual relations but also on the moral issues: the relation of sex to love, responsibility, and personal concern, the danger of "recreational" sex—and the ways in which the AIDS virus is transmitted, as well as protective measures against infection.

Conservative religious groups may protest that a program of sex education in middle and secondary schools is not proper since it only encourages promiscuity. But they are blinded to the fact that our teenagers are already saturated with sex education by TV and the movies that celebrate the rapture of sensual enjoyment. The real question then becomes not *whether* students should have sex education but, rather, *when* and *what kind* of sex education should they have?

The AIDS epidemic, the high incidence of venereal diseases, as well as the marked increase in teenage pregnancies in the last few decades, have prompted federal and state agencies and local school boards to give serious attention to sex education programs at both the secondary and primary levels. The guidelines proposed are strongly normative. As a pamphlet of the National Education Association puts it, "Health education that relies only on the transmission of information is ineffective. Behavioral change results only when information is supported by shared community values that are powerfully conveyed." Students should know the facts about semen, ovaries, menstruation, etc., yes, "but we must remember it is their sense of right and wrong, their internal moral compass, that determines their actions. Sex education then should teach about sex in a way that emphasizes the reasons for abstinence, restraint, responsibility, ... that sexual intimacy is more than merely a physical or mechanical act."[7]

Should information about condoms and other contraceptives be included? Former Surgeon General Everett Koop encouraged their wider availability as one protection against AIDS for those who *do* engage in sexual activity with partners who may be infected with the virus. Religious conservatives protest that condoms should not be publicized and made more

46

available "over the counter." The NEA guidelines point out that "the use of condoms can reduce but by no means eliminate the risk of contracting AIDS . . . . The best way . . . is to refrain from sexual activity until as adults they are ready to establish a mutually faithful monogamous relationship."[8] The North Carolina Board of Education guidelines encourage abstinence, but acknowledge the need for prudence in the use of condoms for those who do engage in premarital intercourse.

These normative guidelines, whether or not heard or heeded by the 15-year-old students in the local high school, reflect the Judeo-Christian ethical tradition of the relationship of sex to love. Sexual activity is not immoral, as viewed in some Puritan stereotypes. It is a wholesome good, but good only when set within the context of moral responsibility of each partner for the other—in short, a caring for the other, which is the Judeo-Christian meaning of love. Apart from this context, sex becomes an expression of lust, the use of another person for one's own physical pleasure. And these, incidentally, are issues that can be addressed in courses of English and American literature.

Drug Abuse

Another part of the health and hygiene curriculum should focus on the problem of drug abuse. As with sexual activity, we described earlier how the use of addictive substances in the schools is now increasing at a perilous rate, whether smoking marijuana, shooting with hard drugs like heroin, LSD, cocaine or its cheaper form crack, or drinking alcohol. According to one recent study, 17 percent of high school seniors have at least tried cocaine.[9] Former Surgeon General Koop has warned that the sharing of drug needles and syringes by those who shoot drugs is the fastest way that the AIDS virus is being spread.[10] The consequences for academic and athletic achievement, especially in the public schools of the inner-city ghetto, are dire. Students frequently spaced-out are likely to drop out of school,[11] take to the streets, and steal money to get drugs. More than half of all adolescent suicides are drug-related. The death toll from automobile accidents in which students are driving drunk or spaced-out is staggering—and should indeed be sobering.

To be sure, this plague is not limited to public schools and colleges. Students in many preparatory schools and private colleges engage in drug trafficking and alcohol abuse. But the parents of these students in the upper economic strata can afford lawyers who can assist their children when in trouble. Unfortunately, the more serious problems appear among the pupils of the schools of the depressed inner cities whose parents cannot afford legal help. And in both situations, the problem may be compounded by the fact that frequently parents and teachers may themselves be caught in one or another form of addiction. In such cases, their children or students are well aware of the hypocrisy of their admonition to say no.

An essential part of a health and hygiene curriculum therefore should not only contain the chemical facts about drugs and alcohol and their effect on the body, but it should also join the battle against their use. Instructors as well as parents should teach pupils by precept as well as by example to say no. Such stern prohibition, of course, may itself be an incitement to sneak "behind the barn" and disobey the mandate. More than a simple prohibition, alternative forms of recreation in athletics, in music, dance, and the arts, can lead young people away from the illusion cultivated by TV commercials that happiness consists in buying the chemical ways to sensate bliss. School recreation programs can enable them to get high in healthy ways. Instructors should teach the principle that everyone is a steward of her or his body and should be responsible for its care in order to remain fit to serve neighbors for whom one is responsible. Such instruction may move out from the classroom to inspire other popular movements similar to SADD (Students Against Drunk Driving), or Project Graduation, which has students pledge themselves to abstain from alcohol or drugs during the ceremonies and festivities surrounding commencement.

Social Studies

Another crucial part of the visible curriculum is social studies, which includes American history, political science or civics, economics, and world cultures. Although these parts of the curriculum move out from the sort of immediate, urgent issues of personal behavior discussed above, they too are permeated with problems of ethical values that affect personal evaluations of students and prepare them for worthy behavior as adult citizens. Teaching and learning American history or civics is not value-neutral. Within the facts are ethical norms about what constitutes a healthy political society.

Former Secretary of Education William Bennett sharply criticized those who set the curricula for our public schools for, among other things, their neglect of the study of history. It is indeed important that students learn the story of our heritage as a nation: the Colonial period, the American Revolution, the establishment of our constitutional structure of government, the development of an agricultural economy that relied on slavery, the crises leading up to the Civil War, the technological revolutions of the industrial era, the two major world wars, the civil rights movement, and now the issues of the postindustrial period. The challenge for teachers is to treat the ethical issues that run through all these periods of our history. For example, when the Massachusetts Bay Colony was established, in part to escape religious persecution in England, was it right for the Puritans to persecute dissenters from their own religious doctrines and to hang to death four Quakers on the Boston Common and to run a Baptist like Roger Williams out of the colony? What is the moral logic of our democratic form of government, as framed in the Constitution, with its separation of powers among the legislative, judicial, and executive branches? What moral spirit makes the exercise of the Bill of Rights viable and protects it from anarchy? Are the freedoms of speech, press, and worship absolute or are there morally legitimate limits to their exercise? Do these restraints come from an inner moral obligation to exercise one's rights with responsibility, to speak and print the truth, and to honor divergent forms of worship, or do they come only from the outer restraints of law? The health of a democratic society, as de Tocqueville pointed out long ago, depends upon the "habits of the heart" of its citizens who can be trusted to exercise their rights responsibly. Therefore moral education is a crucial part of the social studies curriculum.[12]

Another part of American history studies is the troubled story of civil rights. The prolonged controversy about the enslavement of Africans and African-Americans, leading up to the Civil War and the freeing of the slaves, has not meant the end of racial strife in America. The battle for human rights for minorities—Native Americans, African-Americans, Asian Americans, Hispanics—pitched against the dominant power of Anglo-Saxons, seems to be endemic to our culture. Here, too, the social studies curriculum should point students to the moral values at stake in this story of our past and present. Our public schools, integrated by law since *Brown v. Board of Education,* can become laboratories in healthy race relations, where white stereotypes of Blacks can be overcome and vice versa, and relations can be shifted from interracial to interpersonal. Or schools can become scenes of racial discrimination and violence. It depends on the conscious effort of students and teachers. It will not suffice for students to learn about the dream of Martin Luther King, Jr. It is also imperative for them to learn about the economic, psychological, and political forces that both aid and prevent Dr. King's dream from becoming a reality.

Social studies also of course includes economics. An important moral issue here has to do with capitalism as the established practice in America. The capitalistic moral creed celebrates the virtues of individual free enterprise, the market economy, competition, materialism, diligence, high consumerism, all personified in the Yuppie image of the successful American. A century ago, Charles Dickens defined and decried the ethos of the rising capitalism of his day with a sharp word: "Each one for himself and God for us all, as the elephant said as he danced among the chickens." Does this capitalistic morality run counter to or does it accord with what constitutes the "good life" according to our religious tradition: sacrifice, social concern, cooperation, service, and simplicity of lifestyle? These ethical questions lie close beneath the surface of the study of economics.

As the dynamics of our economy leads to the steady rise in the cost of living, more and more parents, father and mother, are employed outside the home to make ends meet. At present, in fewer than one-third of two-parent family households is the husband the sole breadwinner. This increases the demand for day-care centers for preschool children, and for more and more in-school care and supervision for children where neither Mom nor Dad is at home. Although this is surely a spin-off benefit of the women's liberation movement, it is a mixed blessing. Family time together at play and work is sharply reduced, with serious negative effects on the moral nurture of children.

Another area of economics where crucial ethical values are at stake is that of American economic practices in the production and consumption of material goods. A secondary school curriculum on economics and social studies might well address not only the empirical facts about how our industrial economy works, but also the moral values involved, including which common economic practices serve to humanize and which have come to dehumanize the human condition. The attempt here would be to try to tune the consciences of students to a lifestyle, in their getting and spending, to true ethical norms.

Obviously, the high school junior is not an IBM executive or a legislator voting on a tax bill. Nonetheless, there are many points in his or her lifestyle where certain ethical issues are joined. One point where our youth are victimized and miseducated is through commercial TV, which they watch for much longer periods of time than they spend on their homework. And what is celebrated in commercial ads is the doctrine of salvation by gadgetry. The life abundant does not mean a life of service and sacrifice. It consists rather in the abundance of material goods, sensual enjoyment, speeding, getting high.

51

"More is better" is an ethical axiom taken for granted. Is it any wonder that high school and even elementary school students are hooked on junk food from fast-food stands, high on cholesterol, low in nutrition, or why so many get hooked on drugs? Another troubling feature of our American lifestyle of "galloping consumption" is our habit of wasting and littering. Just look at the floor of the high school basketball stadium after the big game. What you see is a microcosm of a national phenomenon—the pileup of solid waste and litter. Nearly 212 million pounds of hazardous toxic waste are produced every day in the United States. Where can it all be dumped to protect our safety and health? Cities are fast exhausting solid waste disposal sites.

In the social studies curriculum as well as in the natural sciences, there are several points where the consciences of students might be schooled and their habits turned toward more responsible ways of consumption. The grounding of such conversion would require a careful look at what has been called "the broken circle": ethics/economics/ecology. That is, the basic norm, derived from the Judeo-Christian covenantal theology, is the norm of stewardship of the earth. The terms of the covenant are that human beings are set in a natural Garden of Eden, "to till and to keep it," as the Bible says; that is, to use the resources of the earth to meet basic human needs. If they abuse and exploit natural resources, violating the covenant, the earth becomes an enemy of human health and life. In the present century we are seeing the dire consequences of such abuse. Deforestation produces soil erosion and bleak deserts. Pollution of the air by carbon monoxide and other pollutants endangers human life. It produces acid rain destroying forests and killing marine life. The greenhouse effect of our pollution of the air makes for lethal smog, reduces the ozone layer, melts the solar ice caps, and raises the sea levels to invade the coastal lines. Through this environmental abuse we are mortgaging the future at a rate that generations following us cannot possibly afford to pay. Unless there is some turnabout in our capital-intensive modes of production and our wasteful habits of consumption, we are headed for ecological disaster. It is imperative in our schooling that these facts be understood and that the next generation be pointed to the ways of closing the broken circle of ethics/economics/ecology.

Although few current materials in the social science curricula give attention to these matters, there are some viable ways to address these issues with corrective knowledge and to cultivate in students an ecological conscience. Students can be shown how to penetrate the cruel fakery of TV consumerism, how to distinguish between real needs and artificial wants. They may be made aware of the ancient truth that a person's true worth does not consist in an abundance of possessions.

In elementary science courses, students can be taught the dynamics of our capital-intensive economy, the difference between renewable and nonrenewable sources of energy, and the problems of toxic waste disposal. Also, in an urban setting, pupils might be enticed to take part in a civic cleanup project or learn where in town are the recycling bins for paper, aluminum, and glass. They might learn about the local Salvation Army or Goodwill Industries centers, where household goods and clothes are recycled, providing employment to the recyclers and sold at moderate prices. If informed about the pockets of poverty across town, students from the more affluent homes might even be led to offer some vacation hours to Habitat for Humanity, a program that builds low-cost housing for the poor by volunteer labor. They might learn, in ways that would bring vividly alive the bare statistics in the economics textbook, about some of the depths of dire poverty in America hidden from sight by the political rhetoric celebrating our freedom and our prosperity. Such a program of social studies would not only inform about the facts, it would also lead students to learn how to use but not abuse the resources of the earth.[13]

The voice of practical realism would interrupt here to point out that many high school students, especially those of lower income background, are forced to look for some kind of part-time jobs in their hours off from school. There is simply no time to give to voluntary community service projects of this sort, even if students were inclined to do so. Yet many social service projects do succeed in capturing the consciences of students.

If the social studies program is confined to American history and culture, however, it may lead students to evaluate policies and lifestyles from a narrow American perspective. Now that the technologies of trade, travel, and communication have made us a global village, increasingly interdependent, students need to learn about other cultures. This has the moral value of widening their outlook from myopic insular nationalism when they discover that America is not the only "land of the free and home of the brave." This involves much more than the study of global geography. Especially at this crucial period of international relations, cross-cultural education becomes a moral imperative. The American Federation of Teachers calls for "more attention to world studies, especially to the realistic and unsentimental study of other nations—both democratic and nondemocratic."[14] The National Education Association continues to promote understanding of global relations in its various publications. And the program of the American Field Service brings students from abroad to American schools. Their presence helps to widen the parochial vision of American students.

Literature and the Arts

Still another part of the visible curriculum where moral education occurs is in the humanities, in the teaching of literature and the arts. In a secondary school course on the classics of Western literature one finds the plays of Shakespeare; the poetry of Chaucer, Milton, John Donne; the novels and essays of Hawthorne, Melville, Thoreau, and Emerson. An astute and sensitive teacher can make the moral dilemmas of the characters in *Hamlet, Macbeth,* or *The Merchant of Venice* contemporary and vivid. The pictures of the good life in Thoreau's *Walden Pond* or Emerson's essays are more than quaint period pieces of a long-gone rural America. They can be taught and studied in ways that reveal their moral relevance for life today. More recent works like *Huckleberry Finn, The Catcher in the Rye* or *The Diary of Anne Frank* all cast in vivid terms the clashes of dark and light, good and evil in the human condition. The works of such African-American writers as Alex Haley, Alice Walker, James Baldwin, and Maya Angelou throw light on the dilemmas of human existence from a Black perspective.[15] An effective teacher can lead students in a literature course to wrestle with the moral dilemmas and resolutions in these works in ways that may genuinely influence their own convictions.

Another valuable tool of moral education is for the English teacher at the secondary school level to teach a course in journal writing. When carefully done and under the terms of confidentiality, students may be led in such writing to probe beneath the superficial record of attending basketball games to the underlying moral problems of interpersonal relations with peers and with parents that bother them deeply. The teacher's responses to journal entries may help students grow in moral sensitivity.

A final problem to address in humanities courses is the teaching of the Bible as literature. In the Supreme Court's *Schempp* decision, Justice Brennan supported the majority opinion permitting the study of the Bible in tax-supported public schools, affirming that in no way does it violate the terms of the First Amendment:

> The holding of the Court today plainly does not foreclose teaching *about* the Holy Scriptures or about the differences between religious sects in literature or history. Indeed, whether or not the Bible is involved, it would be impossible to teach meaningfully many subjects in the social sciences or the humanities without some mention of religion.[16]

A current controversy rages about how the Bible should be taught. Fundamentalists contend that the whole of the Bible is inerrant literally, scientifically true from Genesis to Revelation, while most biblical scholars would distinguish between the poetic and mythological aspects of biblical materials and those that speak in empirical terms of fact. The literalist runs into some puzzling problems: Did Adam have a navel? Was Eve actually created out of Adam's rib? Was the world created in seven 24-hour days? How could two of every animal species of the world be possibly squeezed into the limited space of Noah's ark?

The resolution of this controversy lies in reading much Bible material as "mythological." This means not as false or phony, but as poetic and graphic imagery that describes the nature of reality in ways that elude the empirical description of a scientist. One need not have to believe that Moses literally climbed Mount Sinai to hear the voice of God mandating the Decalogue to acknowledge the moral authority of the Ten Commandments. The moral norms of covenant theology can be conveyed to students in a course on the Bible as literature without their being indoctrinated into the fundamentalist faith that the Bible is inerrant.[17]

In sum, as soon as students have acquired the basic skills of reading, writing, and arithmetic, the moral issues to be found within the facts of health sciences, social sciences, and the humanities can be addressed to help educate their consciences and conduct. Ethics is a requisite element in any educational program concerned about equipping students for responsible citizenship in a humane society.

NOTES

1. See C. Ellis Nelson, *Don't Let Your Conscience Be Your Guide,* (New York: Paulist Press, 1978).

2. See C. Ellis Nelson, ed., *Conscience: Theological and Psychological Perspectives* (New York: Newman Press, 1973) for a thorough treatment of the complexity of the phenomenon of conscience.

3. William Perkins, *Works* (London, 1606), p. 511.

4. The famous studies of Hartshorne and May, *Studies in the Nature of Character,* vol. 1, *Studies in Deceit* (New York: MacMillan,

1928) confirm this Pauline truth about the behavior of children. See also Aronfreed, J., "The Acquisition of Conscience" in C. M. Beck, B. C. Crittenden, and E. V. Sullivan, eds., *Moral Education: Interdisciplinary Approaches* (Toronto: University of Toronto Press, 1971); and "Internal Morality," chap. 5 of Norman Bull, ed., *Moral Education* (Beverly Hills, Calif.: Sage Publications, 1969).

5. Colin Campbell, address to entering class at Wesleyan University, September 1987.

6. U.S. Department of Education, *A Guide for Parents and Teachers: AIDS and the Education of Our Children* (Washington, D.C.: Government Printing Office, October 1987), p. 5. See also U.S. Department of Health and Human Services, *Understanding AIDS* (Washington, D.C.: Government Printing Office, 1988).

7. National Education Association, *The Facts About AIDS* (Washington, D.C.: National Education Association, 1987).

8. Ibid. Another source of information is SIECUS (Sex Information and Education Council of the U.S.), New York University. The Ford Foundation has supported a "family-life education" curriculum in New Jersey public schools (*Ford Foundation Newsletter,* June 1986). These guidelines were set by the North Carolina Board of Education, for instructional use to combat the spread of AIDS: "The three means recommended for young people to protect from AIDS in order of effectiveness and curricular emphases are:

1. Abstaining from sexual intercourse and abstaining from intravenous drugs.
2. Maintaining a lifelong monogamous sexual relationship. . . .
3. Using condoms for protection during sexual activity.

"It is the responsibility of teachers to assure that all students are aware that abstinence is the only sure way to avoid AIDS. . . . However, because AIDS is a deadly communicable disease, it is also necessary that students be familiar with the other, less effective, less desirable means of protecting themselves from AIDS."

9. U.S. Department of Education, *Schools Without Drugs* (Washington, D.C.: Government Printing Office, 1986).

10. U.S. Department of Health and Human Services, *Understanding AIDS*, p. 6.

11. U.S. Department of Education, *Schools Without Drugs*, p. 4. In 1988, the *national* rate of students who dropped out of high school was above 40 percent. The rate is much higher in the inner-city ghetto schools.

12. See American Federation of Teachers, *Education for Democracy*, (Washington, D.C.: American Federation of Teachers, 1987). This publication, while protesting religious indoctrination, acknowledges that the study of American government and society should include "the religious beliefs that have shaped our values and our culture" (p. 16).

13. See Carnegie Commission Report, *Turning Points*, pp. 70–74.

14. Ibid., p. 20.

15. See, for example, Scholastic Literature Anthologies, *A Collection of Prose and Poetry on the Theme of Values*, Michael Spring, ed. (New York: Scholastic, 1987), which contains brief pieces ranging from Sara Teasdale and Mahatma Gandhi to Martin Luther King, Jr., and Andy Rooney. See also the *Annuals of the Society of Christian Ethics* (Washington, D.C.: Georgetown University Press, 1988): *Works of Art and Literature Used in Ethics Courses: An Annotated Bibliography*.

16. *Abingdon Township School District v. Schempp* (374 U.S. 203, 1963).

17. Roland Frye, ed., *Is God a Creationist? The Religious Case Against Creation-Science* (New York: Scribners, 1983). See also Nicholas Pietascalzi and William Collie, eds., *Teaching About Religion in Public Schools* (Niles, Ill.: Argus, 1977), part 2.

Chapter 5

THE HIDDEN CURRICULUM: THE MORAL CLIMATE OF THE PUBLIC SCHOOLS

The previous chapter addressed the issue of how students can be ethically educated through the visible curriculum, that is, in the prescribed materials taught and studied. The assumption here is that more than facts and data are taught. From the physical and life sciences to the social sciences and humanities, value issues are also exposed and explored. It is impossible, indeed irresponsible, for teachers or texts to stay value neutral. In teaching literature, or hygiene, or economics, instructors ought to cultivate in their students not only an awareness of the moral dimensions of each subject but also, it is to be hoped, a sense of moral responsibility in caring for their own bodies and those of others, in preserving the resources of the good earth, and in maintaining a civil and humane society in economic and political practices.

Yet just as significant as the visible curriculum is the "hidden" curriculum. This has to do not with *what* is being taught but *how* the teaching and administration go on in terms of the interpersonal relationships, both inside and outside the classroom, among teachers, administrators, guidance counselors, and athletic coaches, with students, and with parents as well. Many analysts of American public schools testify that this moral atmosphere of the whole school is even more influential in determining moral attitudes and behavior than the materials in the textbooks and classroom instruction.

In teacher-pupil relationships, as the old saying goes, "Example teaches better than precept. One gives a better sermon with one's life than with one's words." Responsible or irresponsible behavior, both in and out of class, may be as much the consequence of the teacher's style and personality as role model as of her or his expertise in the subject being taught and skills in communication.

Here, for example, is the 10-year-old boy who carries from home to class the dark troubles of a breakup between his mother and father. He has not done the assigned homework. He sits in a surly sulk. Or here is a young boy who has visible bruises on his neck and arms, quite apparently from child abuse. Or here the guidance counselor meets with a 14-year-old girl from a broken home who has been "sexually active," sleeping around with several boyfriends. Having missed two menstrual periods, she learns from the medical clinic that she is pregnant. She doesn't know who the father is. What should she do? What advice should the counselor give? Or here is a girl in the fifth grade whose poor reading skills may signal a case of dyslexia. Here is another boy who stutters. A teacher's sensitivity to such traumas and troubles becomes crucial. It may be that the teacher can help that student by a kind word of encouragement or sympathy. Or perhaps the teacher should refer these problems to the school guidance counselor or to the principal or should make an attempt to consult with the parents. A teacher who ignores the smell of alcohol or pot enables the youth to continue down a dangerous road. Letting the student get by with it may be seen by the student as condoning or encouraging that kind of behavior.

We confront here two problems of enormous complexity that make the realization of this ideal of individual personal concern very difficult.

One is simply a quantitative problem: the sheer size of the school. In the large high school of the inner city, individualized personal concern of administrators, counselors, and teachers becomes next to impossible. According to the Carnegie Council report, "it is common for guidance counselors in middle grade schools in this country to be responsible for 500 or more students."[1] The English teacher in the 11th grade will have contact with a class of 30 or 40 pupils for 50 minutes a day, for five days. Each teacher has approximately 150 students. However personally sensitive the teacher may be and however alert to such problems as mentioned above, how can s/he possibly relate to this transient traffic on a one-to-one basis? The specialization of function and the bulk of the school size leads one educational expert to conclude that "large bureaucratic high schools tend to produce a moral atmosphere conducive to disciplinary break-down."[2] The old one-room schoolhouse has long since disappeared from rural as well as urban America. Even the term "homeroom" is a euphemism. It has little of the warm supportive atmosphere of a home. Middle schools are now attempting to return to this small group setting with "home base," but it usually meets, at most, 30 minutes a day.

The other problem that makes ethical education in the public high schools difficult is that by the time students are enrolled in primary and secondary schools, their patterns of moral behavior have largely been set, in the right or wrong direction, by their nurture at home or lack thereof. Teachers and child guidance counselors affirm that the home background is the crucial determining factor in setting value standards for behavior expectations. The school becomes, then, the setting where these standards of civil behavior are refined and internalized, or corrected when the home from which the child comes has cultivated false values. As one scholar of education in America has put it, "moral education is too big a job for schools to tackle alone. Parents are indispensable partners in that enterprise and remain so throughout adolescence."[3] The writer goes on to show how parents can foster mutual respect, help children assume responsibilities, balance independence and control, sustained in all these efforts by an attitude of love and concern.

This normative ideal of the nurture of morality at home, as prior and concurrent with ethical education in school, is certainly correct. This ideal, however, is by no means practiced in all homes. The harsh statistics about the high rate of divorced and separated families, the socioeconomic centrifugal forces pulling the family apart so that its members neither work nor play together, the incidence of violent child abuse, as well as of alcoholism and drug abuse on the part of parents—all make this ideal in many cases a romantic fantasy, particularly in impoverished inner-city households. When children come into school with a value scheme skewed by their home backgrounds, it becomes very difficult for the school to set it aright. The problem is further compounded by the fact that at adolescence the peer pressure of the gang or clique becomes a dominant influence in determining behavior. Very often what the peer group is doing runs counter to what parents or teachers may expect or demand.[4] Teenagers would rate in the following order of priority the factors that influence their values: (1) peers, (2) the media, (3) family, and (4) other adult figures.

Despite these obstacles, through the hidden curriculum all aspects of school life beyond the instructional material of the classroom can nonetheless influence the behavior of students and cultivate in them integrity, a responsible concern for others, and orderly behavior. These "habits of the heart" have to do with the voluntaristic or affective side of the educational process, rather than the cognitive—with the heart, not the mind. Nurture into responsible citizenship has both negative and positive features: the discipline and constraints on disruptive behavior and concurrently the positive corrective strategies of cultivating a social conscience.

ETHICAL NORMS FOR DISCIPLINARY PROBLEMS

Consider first the negative aspects. We can readily dismiss the image of the moral innocence of school children, even those from stable homes where caring parents have tried to lead their children into responsible behavior. Students in a typical 11th grade class are not all models of propriety and decorum. The propensity for mischief, like original sin, has been present among the young since the days of Cain and Abel. Many rough incidents of misconduct go on every day, in and out of the classroom: physical violence in the hall or in the school yard during recess, stealing, sexual assaults, mutilation of school property, or painting raw graffiti on the school walls or in restrooms. And as noted earlier, drug trafficking and use are increasing ominously, especially with alcohol and crack.

What ethical norm should guide policy and practices for teachers or administrators in dealing with disruptive behavior? A policy of complete permissiveness by school authorities, allowing any and all kinds of disruptive conduct, would be irresponsible to the moral purposes of education. The norm of *fairness* in disciplinary action, where the severity of punishment is proportionate to the seriousness of the offense, is an accepted ethical principle of law and should also guide school policy. As one school counselor observed, "Students will support a strict, fair teacher more readily than an easy, unfair teacher." It is general practice for schools to issue student handbooks spelling out the rules of community relations, specifying student rights and responsibilities, and indicating in detail the punishments for disruptive or dangerous behavior.[5] Nonviolent offenses such as repeated tardiness or skipping class may be punished by in-school suspension (sending a student to another monitored schoolroom for study, isolated from peers for a day). More serious offenses such as abusive language, vandalism, or the possession of weapons or drugs often result in out-of-school suspension or expulsion. Corporal punishment is not usually allowed; but in some school districts it is permitted only in certain carefully specified circumstances.[6] By and large, however, the practice of corporal punishment in most school systems of the nation is not allowed, for evidence shows that the consequence of such a form of punishment does not prove to be corrective. It only increases the proclivity to habits of violence and disruption.

A policy that steers a careful course between complete permissiveness and physical abuse is what fairness in retributive justice requires and may lead offending students to mend their ways.

Just as in courts of law, it is impossible in school behavior codes to specify in every detail where fairness in disciplining misbehavior should be stern and where lenient. Yet one element is certainly an ethical norm: fairness in punishment means a flexibility that takes into account the vast range of differing personal circumstances, the handicaps, merits, and needs of the student. It means also that the punishment imposed should never discriminate according to the racial, ethnic, or religious background of any student.

Given the range of variables in any one school setting, it is always difficult to be completely fair. A recent incident in a public school in the so-called Bible belt may illustrate the dilemma. Three young children from an ardent Christian fundamentalist family were "preaching" at the gates of a small elementary school yard, waving their Bibles, shouting verses about whoremongers and fornicators. The oldest, age 11, refused to enter the school and was suspended for a brief period in the spring. At the opening of the school year in the fall, when he resumed his street preaching and told the principal to "go to hell," the boy was suspended for 10 days. The boy's father came to his defense with this statement:

> The issue here is God and the devil. The gods of the public school system are Horace Mann and John Dewey. Their religion is this: humanism, evolution, integration. That's why they don't want the kids promoting the King James Bible around the school anywhere.[7]

Was the disciplinary action of the principal in suspending the student a violation of his constitutional right to the free exercise of religion? After all, recent court decisions have allowed religious groups of whatever persuasion to hold meetings after school hours on school grounds. Yet the boy's defiance of school authorities in word and action certainly warranted some kind of punishment for his disruptive and disrespectful behavior. It is to be hoped that, out of this experience (if in the procedure exacting this punishment he was treated with dignity and respect), he might have come to realize that he was punished for his defiance of authority, not for his religious beliefs.

POSITIVE STRATEGIES FOR IMPROVING MORAL BEHAVIOR

The cultivation of conscience and responsibility does not follow alone from the negative policies of punishment we have just outlined, however fairly administered. There are positive measures in the hidden curriculum that are more constructive.

One is a systemic change in the school organization and structure that would reduce the average class size for teachers, thus affording more opportunity for one-on-one teacher-pupil relationships, and the opportunity for the expression of personal concerns to the variant problems and needs of each student in the classroom. This is a tall order, given the current budgetary constraints on public schools that are suffering cutbacks in federal, state, and county funding and the shortage of teachers, a factor largely due to low salaries. Yet this fiscal and systemic change, to alter the teacher/pupil ratio and to provide for ethically conscientious guidance counselors, is a prerequisite to creating more sensitive and responsible community relations in the public school, whether large or small.

A second positive strategy, similar to the first, is the practice of the norm of participatory democracy. School administrators develop small group "town meetings," rap sessions where students and teachers engage in discussions and learn about problems such as drug abuse, vandalism, AIDS, the terms of an honor code, factors affecting the high or low dropout rate, the sports program. One such pilot program that was carried on in a large inner-city high school with a faculty of 200 and a student enrollment of 2,000 had definite positive results. It improved student attitudes and behavior in racial and ethnic relations, the protection of school property, and academic achievement.[8]

A third measure of proven benefit is the fruit of a close relation of school and home, of teachers and administrators with parents. This involves something more than the cordial monthly PTA meeting with cider and doughnuts. It requires a conscientious effort on the part of school faculty and staff to consult with parents in a joint effort to deal with the particular foibles and quirks of students, to encourage parents in setting high goals of accomplishment, to monitor what their children watch on TV, to help with homework, etc. True, many homes are single-parent homes, but there is nothing in such situations to prevent the single mother—or father—from working together with the school in the moral nurture of the child.

A fourth factor influencing the moral atmosphere of the school for good comes from the extracurricular activities that lift morale and give students a sense of pride and loyalty to the school community. This again has to do with the affective aspect of education, rather than the cognitive. It means more than just having a lively group of bouncing cheerleaders at basketball games, waving pompoms, heartening as that may be to the team. More significant are programs that create a sense of community, that recognize the fine qualities of personal character—for example, election to the National Honor Society or granting Merit Scholarships, or developing peer-counseling programs of older students to tutor younger students in their course work or personal problems of adjustment. The earlier mentioned SADD program (Students Against Drunk Driving) can bring corrective peer pressure to bear on the problem of alcohol use. The athletic program can be a crucial area where interpersonal relations between coaches and athletes can cultivate integrity in sportsmanship and a spirit of fair play.

In previous epochs of American education, the sense of moral accountability and community loyalty was nurtured and sustained by the regular weekly assemblies. The inclusion of prayer and scripture reading in school assemblies prevailed in the public as well as the private schools well into this century. More recently, separationist interpretations of the First Amendment by the courts have ruled such practices out of bounds. Although there is a strong tide of public opinion favoring the restoration of daily prayer in public schools, for the most part school assemblies are secular in content. With or without prayer, however, assemblies that raise issues of moral concern, that recognize students of character and quality, do create a sense of school pride and personal responsibility.

Finally, community service projects provide excellent educational opportunities for students to be turned away from a me-centered ethos (or "me-itis"). The minds and hearts of this generation are taught by the mass media to derive maximum physical self-satisfaction through high consumerism. Most students in the average middle-class suburban community are unaware of the needs of the poor across town or in areas of desperate poverty in South and Central America and Africa. Many examples can be cited of programs that develop an ethos of responsible citizenship. For example, a condition of admission to the tax-supported North Carolina School of Science and Math is a commitment to perform 60 community service hours per summer and 3 school community service hours per week during the school year. And in the judicial system, courts are sentencing more and more adolescent offenders to perform community service.

In any community, students can be led to overcome their moral myopia by participating in civic or church-sponsored programs and drives that serve the needs of the poor, that can protect the natural environment, that provide basic health resources for those nearby and those far away. They can give blood to the Red Cross, take part in the annual Walk for World Hunger, sell Girl Scout cookies, offer time on weekends to the local soup kitchen or the overnight shelter for the homeless, visit the elderly in the nursing home or the pediatric clinic at the local hospital, volunteer to work with the crew building low-cost homes in the Habitat for Humanity program. Or they can help organize a neighborhood project that recycles glass and paper to conserve the dwindling resources of the earth. To be sure, in many situations voluntary community service on the part of high school students is made very difficult or precluded by harsh economic constraints. Students have to have part-time jobs to help with a meager family income. Nonetheless, in many households there are teenagers who can be turned from dangerous habits through community service.

All these activities, whether carried on under school, church, or civic auspices, provide an opportunity for students of whatever economic level, to learn how much they owe to society, to develop a social conscience, and to translate the promptings of that conscience into concrete action.

NOTES

1. Carnegie Council on Adolescent Development, *Turning Points,* p. 40.

2. Clark Power, "Democratic Moral Education in the Large Public High School," in Marvin W. Berkowitz and Fritz Oser, eds., *Moral Education: Theory and Application* (Hillsdale, N.J.: Lawrence Erlbaum, 1985), pp. 219 and ff. The research here is based on the study of Brookline (Mass.) High School.

3. Thomas Lickona, "Parents as Moral Educators," chap. 5 in Berkowitz and Oser, *Moral Education,* p. 144.

4. See the classic studies of Erik Erikson, *Childhood and Society* (New York: Norton, 1950), and *Identity, Youth, and Crisis* (New York: Norton, 1968).

5. See for example, Guilford County (N.C.) School System, *Student Handbook, 1988–89* or *Student Handbook for Durham County Schools* (1988–89).

6. Guilford County *Handbook,* p. 25. The rules here are that corporal punishment may be administered only "in the presence of a second school official, . . . that only reasonable force should be used . . . never administered by a principal or teacher when angry . . . and administered in privacy."

7. *Durham Morning Herald* (Durham, N.C.), August 23, 1988.

8. See Power, chap. 9 in Berkowitz and Oser, *Moral Education.*

SELECTED BIBLIOGRAPHY

American Federation of Teachers. *Education for Democracy.* Washington, D.C.: American Federation of Teachers, 1987.

Beck, C. M.; Crittenden, B. S.; and Sullivan, E. V., eds. *Moral Education: Interdisciplinary Approaches.* Toronto: University of Toronto Press, 1971.

Bellah, Robert, et al. *Habits of the Heart: Individualism and Commitment in American Life.* San Francisco: Harper and Row, 1985.

Berkowitz, Marvin, and Oser, Fritz, eds. *Moral Education: Theory and Application.* Hillsdale, N.J.: Lawrence Erlbaum, 1985.

Carnegie Council on Adolescent Development. *Turning Points: Preparing American Youth for the 21st Century.* Washington, D.C.: Carnegie Corp., June 1989.

Damon, William. *The Moral Child: Nurturing Children's Natural Moral Growth.* New York: Free Press, 1988.

Department of Health and Human Services. *Illicit Drug Use, Smoking and Drinking by America's High School Students, College Students, and Young Adults: 1975–1987.* Publication No. (ADM) 89–1602. Washington, D.C.: Government Printing Office, 1989.

Dykstra, Craig. *Vision and Character: A Christian Educator's Response to Kohlberg.* Ramsey, N.J.: Paulist Press, 1981.

Elias, John. *Moral Education, Secular and Religious.* Malabar, Fla.: Robert E. Krueger Publishing Co., 1989).

Erikson, Erik. *Insight and Responsibility.* New York: Norton, 1964.

Ferkiss, Victor. *The Future of Technological Civilization.* New York: George Braziller, 1974.

Gilligan, Carol. *In a Different Voice.* Cambridge: Harvard University Press, 1982.

Giroux, Henry, and Purpel, David, eds. *The Hidden Curriculum and Moral Education: Deception or Discovery.* Berkeley: McCutchan Publishing Corp., 1983.

Gow, Kathleen M. *Yes, Virginia, There Is Right and Wrong.* New York: John Wiley and Sons, 1980.

Hall, Robert, and David, John V. *Moral Education in Theory and Practice.* Buffalo: Prometheus Books, 1975.

Hayes, C. D., ed. *Risking the Future: Adolescent Sexuality, Pregnancy, and Childbearing.* (Washington, D.C.: National Academy Press, 1987.

Joy, Donald M., ed. *Moral Development Foundations: Judeo-Christian Alternatives to Piaget/Kohlberg.* Nashville: Abingdon Press, 1983.

Keniston, Kenneth, and Carnegie Council on Children. *All Our Children: The American Family Under Pressure.* New York: Harcourt Brace, Jovanovich, 1977.

Kohlberg, Lawrence. *Essays on Moral Development.* Vols. 1 and 2. San Francisco: Harper and Row, 1981, 1984.

Kohlberg, Lawrence, and Triel, L. *Moralization Research: The Cognitive Developmental Approach.* New York: Holt, Rinehart, and Winston, 1971.

Lasch, Christopher. *The Culture of Narcissism.* New York: Norton, 1978.

McClelland, David C., ed. *Education for Values.* New York: Irvington Publishers, 1982.

National Commission on Excellence in Education. *A Nation at Risk.* Washington, D.C.: Government Printing Office, 1986.

Peters, R. S. *Ethics and Education.* Keystones of Education Series. New York: Scott, Foresman and Co., 1966.

Purpel, David. *The Moral and Spiritual Crisis in Education: A Curriculum for Justice and Compassion in Education.* Granby, Mass.: Bergin and Garvey, 1988.

Purpel, David, and Ryan, Kevin, eds. *Moral Education: It Comes with the Territory.* Berkeley: McCutchan Publishing Corp., 1976.

Roszak, Theodore. *Where the Wasteland Ends.* New York: Doubleday, 1972.

Scharf, Peter, ed. *Readings in Moral Education*. Minneapolis: Winston Press, 1978.

Sichel, Betty. *Moral Education: Character, Community and Ideals*. Philadelphia: Temple University Press, 1988.

Simon, Sidney, et al. *Values Clarification*. New York: Hart, 1972.

Spring, Michael, ed. *A Collection of Prose and Poetry on the Theme of Values*. New York: Scholastic, 1987.

Straughan, Roger. *Can We Teach Children to Be Good?* London: George Allen, 1982.

Sugarman, Barry. *The School and Moral Development*. New York: Harper and Row, 1973.

Toffler, Alvin. *Future Shock*. New York: Random House, 1970.

U.S. Deptartment of Education. *AIDS and the Education of Our Children*. Washington, D.C.: Government Printing Office, October 1987.

Westby-Gibson, Dorothy. *Social Perspectives on Education*. New York: John Wiley and Son, 1965.

Journals dealing with issues of Moral Education:

Daedalus (Journal of the American Academy of Arts and Sciences)
Ethics, Easier Said Than Done (published by the Josephson Institute for the Advancement of Ethics)
Journal of Moral Education
Religious Education